FOUND IN A LETTER 1959

Ex Ophidia Press

Found in a Letter 1959

"Brava, Sharon Cumberland, for *Found in a Letter 1959*, an original and inventive collection based on a trove of her father's actual letters that chronicle the family's life stories from her Dad's military service and beyond. With wit and resourcefulness, Cumberland has found a worthy voice to inhabit in her father's often eloquent letters to his dying father, revealing a plethora of evocative, midcentury markers: slide rules, Martini parties with pigs in a blanket, measles, lipstick, Shalimar! These poems are a witness to history — her own as well as midcentury America's. This book is nothing short of marvelous."

– Nancy Schoenberger,
The Fabulous Bouvier Sisters

"I've never read anything like this: the way Cumberland blends past, present, and future so we feel the distinct temperatures as well as one cohesive environment — an impressive feat. I read this collection in awe of how such emotional knowledge is developed, and I also left the poems wounded by and reminded of the sexism that still seeks to limit a woman's power and independence in daily life — especially in military culture. These letters and poems, carefully planted within the landscape of 1959, create a portrait of courage, vulnerability, wartime recovery, and above all, the complicated beauty of family."

– Abby E. Murray,
Hail and Farewell

"Sharon Cumberland may have invented a new lyric form, composed of monologues in her father's voice interwoven with passages from his letters written as a naval serviceman in World War II and as a Sloane Fellow at M.I.T. in 1959. What emerges is the portrait of an ordinary man of his times, imbued with a quiet, steady, often poignant heroism."

– Gardner McFall,
The Pilot's Daughter

Strange with Age

"Cumberland's poems are clear as a river and cold to the teeth — the poems are so personal it almost seems indecent to show them. How truer a picture they are than X-ray or photo."
                                                        – Sandra Cisneros

Strange with Age, for all its formal and lyrical feats — and there are many, including a deft and moving crown of sonnets for an aging father — is more than the sum of its fine parts. It is proof that wisdom — the real, hard-earned kind, built of experience, intelligence, faith, and yes, age — does not take the place of desire, but stands arm-in-arm with it, offering truth, consolation, and a lovely sense of humor."
                                                        – Kathleen Flennikin

"In these poems, Sharon Cumberland explores grief, the difficulties of faith and doubt, the inescapable movement of time and many aspects of the everyday and the extraordinary. A reader leaves this book feeling a little more familiar with the strangeness of age, as well as reinvigorated about what narrative poetry can do in the hands of a talented artist."
                                                        – Tod Marshall

"Sharon Cumberland gives us visionary poems in the broadest and deepest sense of the word. Their sensory impact is immediate and unforgettable: after traveling with her poems for a while, we smell 'apple tobacco flavoring the air,' we see the trees from a fresh perspective: 'They grow every day at a pace we can't notice. Trees do not act: they are acted upon.' Famous people are made accessible: the poet's parents knew Picasso, her brother met Eisenhower, and Jesus himself instructs us like a mysterious rabbi. By the time I finished reading *Strange with Age*, I, too, was ready to 'drop my jug, snatch up / my life, run to town / filled with good news.'"
                                                        – Lyn Coffin

Peculiar Honors

"Sharon Cumberland knows the forceful pronouncement, but also possesses the rarer gift for quietness and gentle naming — a contemporary Adam christening the hard-to-name emotions and perceptions of grief, happiness, faith."

– Andrew Hudgins

"Sharon Cumberland's exquisitely crafted poems explore passion and love, death an grief. The death of a child — her nephew — and her path toward the sacred form the leitmotifs in the collection, punctuated by flashes of genuine humor. She can be very funny as well as deadly serious – and sometimes, brilliantly, both at the same time."

– Judith Roche

"In these poems we meet Madonnas in jeans; Athenas in Greek widow's weeds; nosey aunts with faces displayed on Mylar birthday balloons; and medieval schoolmasters enjoining their pupils to write themes on those who have died by drowning, crucifixion, or pure joy."

– Carolyne Wright

"Cumberland's eyes and heart miss nothing, whether considering the worried magi in the nativity story, two mortal raccoons 'big as small gondolas,' or 'that thief, who let my hair grow / gray without him.'"

– Gardner McFall

FOUND IN A LETTER 1959

A MEMOIR IN POEMS

SHARON CUMBERLAND

EX OPHIDIA PRESS
2022

The poet wishes to thank the members of the
Greenwood Poets of the Greenwood Senior Center
in Seattle, Washington, whose companionship,
faithful reading, and wise suggestions
are greatly appreciated.

The poet would also like to thank her family,
who inspired these poems,
with special thanks to her beloved husband,
James T. Jones,
for his artistry, editing, and encouragement.

"Sunday Morning before Church" was originally published
in *Strange with Age* (Black Heron Press, 2017).

Cover art and design: Josef Venker, S.J.
Format design: Richard-Gabriel Rummonds
Production: Marcia Breece
Image: United States Naval Academy insignia,
Class of 1944

Published by
Ex Ophidia Press
17037 10th Avenue NE
Shoreline, WA 98155
exophidiapress.org

ISBN: 978-1-7373851-2-7

Dedicated to the descendants of
John Iseman Cumberland Jr.
(1921-2017)

John Iseman Cumberland Jr.

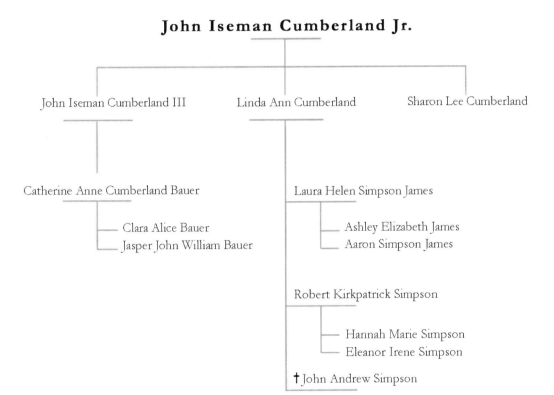

John Iseman Cumberland III   Linda Ann Cumberland   Sharon Lee Cumberland

Catherine Anne Cumberland Bauer   Laura Helen Simpson James

— Clara Alice Bauer
— Jasper John William Bauer

— Ashley Elizabeth James
— Aaron Simpson James

Robert Kirkpatrick Simpson

— Hannah Marie Simpson
— Eleanor Irene Simpson

† John Andrew Simpson

Names in the Poems

Jack — John Iseman Cumberland Jr. (letter writer, 38 years old)

Dad/Cumbie — John Iseman Cumberland Sr. (Jack's father, 59 years old)

Mom/Mother — Opal Hotson Cumberland (Jack's mother, 59 years old)

Grandad/Grandaddy — Henry Cumberland Sr. (Cumbie's father, Jack's grandfather, 83 years old)

Ree — Marie Cumberland (Jack's wife, 37 years old)

John — John Iseman Cumberland III (Jack and Ree's son, 14-15 years old)

Linda — Linda Ann Cumberland (Jack and Ree's daughter, 12-13 years old)

Sharon — Sharon Lee Cumberland (Jack and Ree's daughter, 10-11 years old)

Henry/Uncle Henry — Henry Cumberland Jr. (Jack's uncle, Cumbie's brother, Henry Cumberland Sr.'s son)

Aunt Catherine/Kitty — Catherine Govereau (Henry Jr.'s wife)

Frank — Frank Padulla (Cumbie's hospital roommate)

Richard — Richard Goldupp (Ree's father)

Ruth Anne — Ruth Anne Perry Cumberland (Jack's third wife)

Bob and Jane Divol — a colleague of Jack's in the Sloan program and wife

Mullaney — USS Mullaney (DD 528, Jack's second destroyer class ship assignment as a lieutenant in World War II)

Bristol — USS Bristol (DD 857, Jack's first destroyer assignment)

Hyman — USS Hyman (DD 732, Jack's third and final destroyer assignment)

Elmer — the family cat

Piney Point — The Goldupps' summer home on the eastern slope of the Chesapeake Bay

Additional proper names are historic figures or public figures from the era of the poems.

About the Form

The *italicized portions of these poems* are the words of my father taken unedited and uncorrected from letters he wrote at two stages of his life:
- The "final letter" he wrote to his wife in 1944 as a twenty-four-year-old naval officer facing death at sea. That letter is reproduced in full in the second section of this book.
- The letters he wrote as a thirty-eight-year-old Sloan Fellow at the Massachusetts Institute of Technology in 1959, when his father was suffering from prostate cancer. Selections from those letters make up the bulk of the second section of this book.

About the Letters

In 1959 Jack's father was in Sibley Hospital in Washington, D.C. with prostate cancer. Jack wrote to his father every day for six months. All the letters are written on his Naval Academy stationary — heavy cream-colored paper with a gold '44 insignia letterhead. The letters reproduced here represent only a small portion of the collection, which can be found in the Sharon L. Cumberland Archive, Special Collections, Morris Library, The University of Delaware.

Although Jack graduated from the Naval Academy in the class of 1944, he and his classmates were hurried through their program and into WWII a year early, in 1943. After the war Jack continued to work for the Navy as a civilian engineer.

In 1959 he was chosen to represent the Navy as a Sloan Fellow at the Massachusetts Institute of Technology (M.I.T.) in Boston for an intensive one-year MA program at the Sloan Business School. That year, Jack, Ree, and their three children, John, Linda, and Sharon, moved from Key West, Florida to Newton Centre, Massachusetts.

CONTENTS

The Poems

The Letters

Ave atque Vale

THE POEMS

In Case of Jack Cumberland Being Reported Missing or Dead

July 6, 1945

I.

My Own Dear Ree:
Although I'll write you more, this is really my last letter to you.
We've spent so much of our time in the mail
that it seems right that I should tell you good bye this way.
I can't say that I don't like writing this
because I've enjoyed every word I have ever written to you.
I am 24 years, 11 months, and 9 days old.
We've been married for 2 years and a month.
Johnny is 1 year and a smidgen.
We left the baby with the folks
and drove across country to Seattle
— a desperate second honeymoon
at The Rhododendron
before I followed my orders,
took Military Air Transport
to the Navy Yard in San Diego.
I didn't feel the need for this the last time out,
but somehow I just feel that this time is it.
I think my luck has run out.
My faith hasn't, though — not by a long shot.
I'm the Gunnery Officer on the USS Bristol (DD 857),
newly commissioned to fight
in the South Pacific. We just stopped over
in Pearl Harbor — My God, what a tragedy —
but back up and fighting, sending us out
headed for Guam, full speed ahead.
It's just that you'll have a long wait here on earth
before we're together again. I ask only one thing of you —
make it a happy wait. I won't tell you how I think you can make it
a happy wait. You're the only one who can know that.
I can tell you what I think is the best way —
marry again. I mean that sincerely.
After all, my darling, are there any limits
to happiness? For all the bravado in the Officer's Mess,
the scat talk in the locker rooms, the bragging
below decks   love is something else,
an ocean of discovery,
safe harbor and high seas all at once.

II.

If you think you've found someone you can be sure of,
then go ahead
since trust is the core of love.
We've trusted each other,
young as we are,
and at war.
Don't do it for Johnny or because I suggest it though.
You've never let a man tell you what to do
once you were old enough
to defy your father —
Do it because of the same full, rich feelings
of body and soul
that first brought us together
once we were older.
When our mothers were buddies
during the Depression — you were just twelve,
me, thirteen — I annoyed the heck out of you
when Aunt Helen brought you to stay
in our little row house in Brookland. Your Dad
was still in Missouri sending money back, your mom
searching for steno work. I read her the Washington Star
aloud at night so she could practice her shorthand,
get a job with my mom at the Department of Justice.
We liked each other better once she got work,
and even better, as we grew — you were always just so —
— your hair like caramel — and you so bright —
And don't believe that those feelings in you
must die with me. Love never dies. We learned that
in Sunday School at Grace Episcopal, where
we were married on graduation day.
I have known your love
and I know how great and capable it is
so tough in love, brave in anger,
tormented — too much drink and history.
Yet I have your love — all in all —
and I'll never have to share it.

III.

Through God we are always together.
If ever you can love again, you'll find me there.
I know about love — the only child
of a Catholic and an Anglican — Grandma Mary
praying me back to Mother Church
while my mother marched me off
to Grace Episcopal. It all sunk in.
Anyone that you could love would have me in him.
I'll always love you, and in God's time we'll be together.
Maybe true love dissolves
into some spirit-cloud when you die
because love stays in the world.
I've often wondered how it would work out in heaven if you
married again. I know now.
The Bristol is pitching as I write this, but I'm calm.
There would be three of us
and I would have the one fast and true friend
I've always lacked here on earth.
You'll marry for both of us. I trust you.

IV.

As much as I long to live
and as much as I long for you,
I don't feel at all bad about leaving.
We've been together since we were kids,
and though it took some time for us to see
each other clearly, love was always
the vapor we moved in.
I pray every night and many times a day
that we may be together safely after the war.
But I feel that I am leaving
and I look forward to it with all the eagerness
and excitement I felt
before I left for the Academy.
I believe in Heaven. I know Jesus is there
with all the saints. I'll join a different kind
of service and work as hard there
as I did here.
I'll just go ahead and wait for you.
Maybe you'll visit me in a dream sometime
before you come for good
or maybe I'll visit you. And if I look different
just remember — the apostles
didn't recognize Jesus
when he came back.
Look at me with your heart.
Dearest Ree, yours is the hard part.
But I don't feel sorry for you,
anymore than I feel sorry for myself.
This love we have is the preview of Heaven.
After the crushing hurt and hopeless loneliness
has been mellowed out by time
when Johnny gets to be three or four,
there'll be many, many things to bring you joy.
Ah, the Bristol is pitching as I write this,
but the clouds are parting.

V.

My life has had everything in it
that a man could ask.
If our love were the only thing in it
it would have been full and rich.
I was surrounded by married folks
all my life, but never suspected
what fused them, what bore them
up and over one challenge
after another. You taught me
the hidden open secret
so astonishing so obvious once
we found it together.
I won't go back over what we've meant
to one another. That would only hurt me now
and you later. We know all we need to know,
the perfection of it, the future of it, our Johnnie.
I've written many more letters
that were longer and better than this
but I've said what I wanted to
and that's what I set out to do.
If I never see you again in this life
just know that
Time is but an empty wall between us
and in His time we will meet like the sky and sea
that merge in a perfect line — *we'll be together as we always have been*
— we only seem to be apart — air, ocean, bodies, heart, horizon —
fused, fathomless, calm — *and shall ever be.*

I love you,
Jack

OCD

January 5, 1959

We got a large bundle of mail today
but it was mostly my Wall Street Journals
and magazines. Mother's card was in the bundle,

though. She must have sent it the minute we
got out of the house. We didn't know the diagnosis
"OCD" in 1959, but "obsessive-compulsive"

sure describes Mother. Every mug had our initials
in red nail polish. Penciled signs were taped
on every shelf: "Peaches" under the cans of peaches.

"Peas" under the peas. When she died, we found everything
labeled in her drawer: "Black calf gloves" on black calf gloves;
"Cotton drawers" on her skivvies. And these letters —

her round hand on every envelope: "I wrote Jack
Thurs. nite." "I answered by airmail postcard Sat.
Jan 10 after Henry and I brot Cumbie home."

Ever since she lost the baby when I was eighteen,
she needed the control of notes and nail polish
to calm the swirl of things in her world.

"Cumbie read the marked portions to Frank Padula."
"Cumbie to grocer on Sat. for tomatoes." "Jack coming Sun."
But we tracked each other like that back then — the weather, ordinary

doings. "Ida and Jim passed thru on their way to Violet's —
brot acorn squash from their garden." Our grandkids think
they invented warbles or tweets or whatever devices they

gab with, but we did it with letters, and Mother
with myriad notes — a parakeet chirping things into submission:
"lipstick," "silver bag," "Jack's anchors" on my dress insignia.

On Patrol

January 5, 1959

It is very cold here with a strong wind blowing.
The policeman on Sharon's patrol post lets her warm up
in his car and even drove her home both times today.

Sharon likes being a patrol so much she gets up
at five in the morning and makes her own
breakfast, puts on two sweaters under her coat

and stands on her post for an hour before anyone
comes. No wonder the officer takes pity on her —
she's got blue lips by the time he gets there.

Her teacher made her the only girl on patrol when a boy
in her class kept sleeping in, so she may be afraid
the same thing will happen to her, even though I promised

to get her up in time. Ree worries, imagines she's too
motivated by honor or anxiety — but I say leave her alone.
Sharon's a Navy brat. She hears the call, salutes, does her duty.

A JOB OF WORK
January 7, 1959

It's a darn shame you had to go back for more work
by Dr. Sterling on the very day we hoped
you would go home. Funny how the word "work"

means something so different when you're sick
than the day-in, day-outness of labor
when you're young and strong and not sick.

After fifty years at Western Union you'd hoped
to lie around reading the papers and smoking
your King Edwards — hoped Mother's illness (we'd all hoped)

would get better, calmer, with your sausages smoking
in the pan and your apron hanging on the nail
by the pantry. Now she's all het up again, smoking

Pall Malls after she'd quit for so long, lying
in bed all day — we're afraid she'll set herself on fire.
She won't do a thing — won't cook, won't go out, lying

when you ask if she paid the bills or how a fire
got started in the begonias. She sure is a job of work
to manage. It's no wonder you got sick
on the very day we hoped you would go home.

JACKPOT
January 7, 1959

Ree and I are more happy than we can say
about your return to the church. We were happy
to hear that Frank did too. The priest must feel

like he hit the jackpot in your room — two
old fallen-aways at once, lying side by side
in narrow iron beds, hands folded over

their last days. Hospitals and conversions
go together. You let Mother raise me
Episcopalian — you didn't care one way

or the other then — but now the ending has begun.
The body that carried you through two wars,
decades at Western Union, and a difficult

marriage is giving in but not up. Still time
to say you're sorry for your bad thoughts, your urges,
those magazines we found hidden in the basement

when we sold the house in 1964, the year
blockbusters took over Brookland
and a fellow mugged you on the front porch.

You and Mother moved to Tucson, leaving
the family history — the boatyard
on F Street, the paper route that took you

to the White House every morning — marooned
in the past. Well, Dad, you're a thing of the past
now too. But the day I wrote that letter, you

and Frank (who knows his story?) and that good old soul,
Father Nameless, like a town crier with his bell
and bad tidings, hit the jackpot
and saved your souls.

Sympathy
January 8, 1959

I know you are glad to hear from me
and I know your days must be terribly long.
Mine are, too, Dad — I'm eighty-nine, twenty
more years than you ever had. I lie awake
listening to my sleepy heart, hoping for daylight —
they have more ways of keeping us alive now
than they had in your time.

But there you were — fifty-nine in 'fifty-nine.
Doctors gave you a year at most. Thank God they were off by ten —
I wasn't ready to be fatherless.
Western Union needed your placid control
of the whole D.C. hub, and Mom — why, she didn't make
a good widow when you finally died. No one could take care of her
as well as you did, though I tried.

I enjoyed my visits with you no end — especially the late evenings
when the hospital was so quiet. I was thirty-eight then with three kids —
Sharon just eleven, Linda near thirteen. In April John turned fifteen.
Ree was so demanding, and M.I.T. expected me to be a Leader of Men —
God knows I needed a break.

The whole world seems to be noisy these days.
Looking back on my trip down I think the visits with you
and Frank did me more good than they did you or Frank.
Nothing short of a dying father would give me an excuse
to spend a day on the road alone — homework on hold, no household
chores, everyone's sympathy.

Dad, you were always so quiet.
You brewed me a demijohn of ginger beer in the basement,
when the prohibition beer jug was empty.
You stewed tough for me and pickled pigs' feet, Mom disgusted upstairs.
You followed my merit badge progress — Star, Life, and Eagle.
Cold mornings you folded papers with me — The Washington Post,
and The Star. You told me stories of Old DC, how you delivered
The Post to the White House, how Grandaddy's boathouse got dredged out
to make the tidal basin, the Jefferson Memorial.
You persuaded Uncle Harold to call in a banker's favor
so Senator Wills would appoint me to Annapolis.

You've been gone now half my life…yet I still hear your high-pitched
laugh, that squeeze on my shoulder before I walk down Newton Street to school.

PIPE

January 8, 1959

I am smoking my new meersham pipe that Ree gave me
for Christmas. It is a real joy. The most surprising thing about it
is the amber bit. The amber bit gives the thing an entirely different

taste. I had heard people say that but it is still a surprise.
I didn't know amber had a taste — probably resin molecules
heat up and mix with the Burley Cavendish or Black Cherry —

it tingles a little on the tongue — mmmm — meerschaum —
the bowl is creamy white, so smooth — like Ree herself —
smells so good, tastes rich, like making love in public

when you can't make love. Just sit in your easy chair
with your feet up after a hard day and make a cloud
of sweet smoke. Boy, oh boy. Sharon likes the smell

too, and the feel of the tobacco. She's learned how to pack
the bowl for me. She does it so well that last week I bought her
a little rosewood pipe of her own. The other kids were a bit

jealous but Ree was furious! I had to put it away until Sharon
is old enough to smoke. She tried it again three years later
when we moved to Italy — anything goes there,

and she was fourteen by then. But she didn't really like it.
Said it was like coffee — smells better than it tastes. Well,
she's just a girl. She'll find out about the simple pleasures

soon enough. Maybe a dad shouldn't say this,
but she looked sexy with that little pipe in her mouth, and her
long hair over one eye like Veronica Lake. Too bad

she doesn't date very much — Ree says she's shy, but how
would I know from the way she emotes around the house?
Ree calls her Sarah Bernhardt. Evidently she's quiet

around the boys at school — but she'd be a waste on them
anyway. Bob Divol called her a heartbreaker the other
day at the picnic and I agree — but can't tell that to Ree.

HOOKEY
January 8, 1959

Last night Ree and I just couldn't keep from playing hookey
and running down to see "Inn of the Sixth Happiness".
It was well worth the stolen time, too. After the morning lecture
on international economics in which we discussed tariffs,

I was convinced that there was not a single unselfish person
in the world, but the gal in that story certainly was.
Here I am learning how to steer the Big Ship of Commerce,
and there she was leading a hundred Chinese children

away from the Japanese invasion. I'm not much like Gladys Aylward,
but we both had to deal with the enemy. I was officer of the deck
when we steamed into Tokyo Bay for the surrender — the biggest
flotilla in history — saved by the A-bomb. I tell Sharon

she might never have been born if we'd had to land. Why,
the enemy would have fought to the death, theirs and mine.
Ree made me throw away my Tokyo souvenirs when we moved —
the combat boot with a separate big toe, the dented helmet.

That gal in the movie led all those kids over the mountains
and now our kids sing "knick-knack paddy-whack,
give a dog a bone" all the time, though Ree
says they just wrote that song for the movie, and the real

Gladys Aylward wasn't as pretty as Ingrid Bergman.
But I'll bet she was beautiful inside. What did she need to know
about international economics? Odd to think that men
in Boston and Washington decide these things. We Sloans

drink martinis at the Faculty Club while missionaries try to feed
kids in China and Africa — even Japan, now the war is over.
We manipulate markets like Eisenhower pushing troop markers
across a war map — not that the people with know-how shouldn't lead,

like the British who created the greatest civil service in the world,
the subject of my thesis. Still — that gal — well, I could learn something
about leadership from her. The professor never talked about the people
in tariff countries — their jobs or children. I guess
that's what movies are for.

14

Blood

January 15, 1959

It just occurred to me that you may not get the card
I wrote yesterday because
I forgot to put the extra
stamp on it.

I also remembered
that I forgot to stop by Red Cross
to pay back the pint of blood we owe them.
I have not given any since leaving Maryland

because there is no bank in Key West
since no one lives there but submariners,
writers hiding in the sun, and the old Conchs —
lobstermen, shrimpers — who don't want

any blood but their own. We never felt
at home there, so much gossip. I couldn't look
sideways at a woman without someone
telling Ree, and she stomping away — as though

there was somewhere to go on an island
two-by-three miles in the Gulf of Mexico.
She'd flee to the movies or the Martello
Towers to glare at the sea — the kids and me

left staring at codfish casserole coagulating
on the glass-top table, then at our feet, like sea
creatures in clear water — anemones, sharks.
The waters were warm but not always safe

for swimming in Key West. Better move
to Boston and M.I.T., where the winters last
forever yet words move slowly through
chill and ice, and the snowflakes so tender.

MEASLES
February 1, 1959

Ree did not feel very well and then I noticed
she had a red rash on her face and neck. It got worse
and all the other symptoms of three day measles

came along with it. The kids think it is very funny.
Role reversal — kids are supposed to get measles
and moms bring them soft-boiled eggs, hot lemonade.

The incubation period, according to Ree's medical
encyclopeadia, is from ten to fourteen days; so
they may not think it is quite so funny in a week or two.

Looking back I don't recall a house full of sickness.
I would have reported it to you, Dad,
and to Mother, who loved those kinds of details —

she who was so sick herself, who never
recovered from being committed to St. Elizabeth's
over the baby who died. Odd to think

I would have had a sister twenty years old in 1959
when our John was fifteen. Instead we have
a memory of a dead baby, hysteria, collapse.

I'm glad I was at Annapolis when it happened.
Sorry you had those grim visits, the dark house
at night, electric shock to authorize, a brain-charged
wife to nurse for the rest of your life instead of a baby girl.

Ree, of course, stayed in bed for a while this morning while the kids
and I went to 9:30 service. The children had a dress rehearsal
for the coronation ceremony of their Gallahad (John)
and Fleur de Leis (Girls) Societies —
an annual ceremony which takes place next Thursday at church.

Purity clubs for young Episcopalians — defunct now, still the thing
in Old Boston then — Knights of King Arthur and all. Ree liked
that kind of thing, the girls in white gowns like little brides,
John in a purple sash.
The kids seemed puzzled, resigned.

TOUGH DINNERS
February 1, 1959

I certainly enjoyed my visit with you.
It was especially good to get out to see Grandad
and to get to see Henry while I was there.

I never called Henry Uncle Henry, or Kitty Aunt Catherine.
I was a respectful boy but an only child — a miniature grown-up
sorting my stamps, serving my Washington Stars,

earning merit badges, brewing the family
beer in the basement. Kids were worker bees
in those Depression days, pulling our weight.

The tough dinners are always a treat —
I finished the last of it as a snack this afternoon.
Depression food — we loved the offal —
the kidneys, livers, sweetbreads, toughs.

Linda was the only one here
who would even take a taste.
— she who surprises us so often with her venturesome
spirit, though awkward sometimes, and shy.
It's because she's tall. She would have been a bolder
boy than her brother.
Well, she made it to Wellesley, got a Ph.D.
in linguistic anthropology from Indiana, wrote a grammar
of an Indian language, got married, divorced, kids.
But back then, as a boy she would have served papers
all over town, made a mint of money, been the president
of everything anywhere she wanted. If she could only
have skipped the boyfriends
and the husband
and been
a boy.

REPORT CARDS

February 6, 1959

This week of studying at home is closer to a vacation
than anything else I have ever done. I have to keep busy,
but you have to keep busy on a vacation, too

painting the trim, repairing the car, mowing the lawn,
putting in the bulbs or digging up the bulbs, rolling up
the winter rug and putting down the summer rug

which is raffia. We mend the little holes with twine
because some kind of critter eats into it each year.
Folks here leave their wool rugs down in summer

I notice, which is funny, as if Christmas is just around
the corner in all that sun. I'm glad we're in a rented house
now. *Our oil burner went on the blink*

last night. It is the landlady's responsibility
so we have a new controller and a new thermostat
at her expense. I have nothing to do but study, study,

study. And handling the kids, of course, and Ree.
And all those parties.

Today is report card day for the whole family. I got all B's
just as I expected. We have to get B's to get our degree
so they are just about in the category of courtesy marks.

It's a business school after all. Sloan fellows are men
coming up in the world so the "gentleman's C" is a B.
There were undoubtedly some A's but it does not mean much.

At the Academy we called those guys "saviors" or "Red Mikes" —
reading all weekend to bone the ratings instead of entertaining drags.
Well, ratings don't count at M.I.T., where you have to be a savior just to get in.

Some of these guys — man alive! I can't get what they're saying
half the time, so I just put my nose to the grindstone and push.
Thought I'd be an admiral someday, but, well, M.I.T. is good enough.

John got a poor report for him. One of his marks was an incomplete
that he will have to make up. He also got a C in Latin, which is greatly
below his capabilities. We expect this from the girls, who aren't as smart

and don't need A's to get married (A's in Latin anyway).
But John is the Cumberland name on parade, into the future,
up the ladder, a step farther than you or I could get, or granddaddy with all

his striving. Still, from stonecutter to mailman to Western Union
to the Naval Academy in three generations — it's all upwards and onwards.
But John, well, *this is not a good year for him and I am looking forward
to getting settled where he can get a firmer start. John needs some stability*
and Ree needs her own home.
The girls, of course, will make do.

Jack and Cumbie (standing)
John, Linda, Sharon on Granddaddy Henry's lap
Cedarhurst, Maryland, July 1948

WRASTLING
February 8, 1959

I have not been feeling too well today and neither has Ree.
We went to our last party before Lent and we ate and drank too much.
Lent means something in this family — always has —
forty days before chocolate Easter eggs and legs of lamb.
Each of us gives something up, dessert, TV, lunchtime martinis.
This year I guess we'll cut back on the partying.

I have been overeating most of the time even without a party,
and then that is usually enough to overdo it. I eat ice cream
right out of the box — a cheap luxury I never had as a kid.
Back then we didn't have the term "chocoholic" —
too close to temperance days not to think "lush" or "drunkard"
with any kind of "holic," Carrie Nation coming at you
with her axe. I'm addicted to chocolate ice cream —
a holdover from the Good Humor man's five-cent Fudgsicle,
my paperboy reward in 1935.

We got to church in fine shape though and we had a big pork
and sauerkraut dinner, so it could not be too bad
(as I always tell myself, until I step on the scale).

We were watching that Pat Boone–Dinah Shore show that Mother
mentioned also. Oh, she loves a crooner, even now — Rudy Valee,
Bing Crosby, shades of her flapper days.

Watching television on the networks is like looking at the moon —
you know people miles away are doing the same thing.
But it doesn't bring you closer like it did in the war, when your sweetheart's
eyes were on the good old moon with yours.

I am afraid we did not see the wrastling since it's so fake —
I don't know how you and Richard can get into that corn.
Andre the Giant is no wrestler — he's as big as a moon, speaking of the moon.
I guess men from the first war get a kick out of fake violence
since the real stuff is too long ago.
The only wrastling I ever watch is when I am with you.

LITERATURE
February 9, 1959

The other class we had today was with Elting Morrison,
who is also the chairman of my thesis committee.

He teaches a course in which he endeavors
to teach us something about the American scene.

He does this by assigning us one book per week
to read, then letting us talk about it. The Scarlet Letter,

The Ox-bow Incident, Letters of Lincoln Steffens. *I dispair*
at our saying anything very educational since

our discussions are generally a mutual exchange
of ignorance. And while I don't dispute the value

of reading about Muckrakers and lynchings, or The Autobiography
of Benjamin Franklin, I wonder what it has to do with me?

We did read Franklin back at McKinley Tech — to make us industrious
I guess — but if it didn't work then, it must be too late now.

Still — since we made it into the Sloane program at M.I.T.
even Franklin would say we're pretty damned industrious,

especially since industry is a lot more complicated for us
than it was for him. Yet I admire old Ben, with his kite

and his key, discovering electricity. Why, in his time
you could make a discovery a day they were so ignorant

of just about everything. Morrison sits in class with a little smile,
amused by a gang of engineers wrastling with literature.

What does he see in us, I wonder? How are we changed?
 Well, *since most of the people in the country are not very well educated either,*

I suppose the very fact that we have taken time to read the books
will be of some value. And now, looking back over these sixty years,

what sticks with me even as my memory goes, is those books,
and that fact that anyone thought it mattered that we read them.

Unsteady
February 12, 1959

I got your Saturday letter and your Monday card.
It is good to hear from you so often. Remember me
to Frank Padula when you see him the next time.

I still can't get over how fate landed you side
by side — like a croupier dealing cards onto a baize
table — or was it God giving you a gift in the midst

of your hard time? *We will have to pay him a visit too*
when we get to Washington to stay. I plan to be very good
about visiting all the people we know there, now that I know

how temporary you are, and Mom, and the neighbors
I grew up with, family friends. Funny how childhood
is permanent — even the trees seem rooted in forever.

You know, Dad, the older I get — the more anchored
I am in marriage and plans — the less steady it all becomes,
as if the currents are shifting my ship off course —

what I thought was a right barque turns into a punt
wheeling circles around the anchor chain.
Sometimes I wonder if the devil is springing

every plank I put down. Just when I get everything
ship-shape and Bristol fashion, something happens —
a fight with Ree, my thesis director on my case,

one kid or the other in trouble, your illness. Remember
when my commander on the Hyman hurt my rating
by saying I worked a problem to "diminishing returns"?

That put the kibosh on my admiral's stripes. Civilian life
was a compromise — what Academy man wants a lubber's
berth? Still, I don't mean to be gloomy. We're young yet,

Ree and I. *We plan to be active in Church and to keep*
our house in good condition. I also want to spend more time
doing things with the kids and helping them

with their education. When you add to this my determination
to do some office work at home, it will probably require
*a forty hour day…*which is one way to hold confusion at bay.

Grandaddy
February 12, 1959

It's too bad Grandaddy is not more at home
out at Carroll Manor. I certainly hope
it is just a time of getting adjusted
and that he will come to enjoy it later on.

He adjusted to everything else
that came down the pike — the death
of a wife, of a daughter, the loss
of work at the shipyard on F Street.

The government built the tidal basin there.
A memorial to Jefferson put him out of business
by right of eminent domain. Grandaddy
salvaged the tools — got his cousins and a mule

and hauled those irons and caulking mallets
right past the gatekeeper. Grandaddy
said the man turned a blind eye, angry
as they all were about turning out hard-working

citizens. Grandaddy cut gravestones, dug foundations,
ended up a mailman on Capitol Hill, Grandma Mary
on his route — proposed to her right on her porch,
mailbag on his shoulder. "I've got two kids

to raise, no time to waste," he said, and so she came
and raised you Catholic. But Mom's Episcopalian.
What a scandal — we know what came of that!
Well, Dad, they say that all's well that ends

well, and Grandaddy will end well yet, you'll see.
He's eighty-three — two decades older than you
will ever be. Carroll Manor, Bell Trace, Harmony
Gardens — all names for heaven's lobby. He'll adjust.

SMALL CITY
February 12, 1959

I am impressed with the smallness
of Washington still. After seeing how many
cities are so large that you can not even phone
out of the neighborhood without

a toll charge. Here in Boston we can not
even call downtown without a message
charge. And soon we will have three teenagers
who live to call the friends they just spent

six hours with in school. Was I like that, Dad,
at Woodrow Wilson, needing to be with
Buddy and George Govereau
like that? I think I was too quiet, not the type

to talk to girls or flirt. Why, we thought
girls were too special, like another
species of creature. You'd wash your hands
to talk to them, and your neck, too.

Mother would have had a conniption if she'd
caught me on the phone — though, sorry —
I didn't mean to say she was out of control.
I know she worked hard to keep it all in.

Well, if you can see me now, Dad, almost ninety
in front of a computer, you wouldn't
give it any credit. I can write to anyone
in the world for free, and phones are so cheap

you can bother people as long as you like.
They carry the phone in their pockets, so
no one can say they're not home. Soon
I'll be with you, Dad, speaking of Home.

GIRLS
February 13, 1959

*John is at Scouts now. Linda is at dancing. Sharon is using John's
microscope set, and Ree is watching TV. I am taking a minute off
from my studies.* The house is quiet. Just the murmur of <u>The Thin Man</u> —
Ree likes a dapper detective. I wonder, was I ever dapper? Am I dapper now?
No — I'm fatter than I've ever been, taking Metrecal, watching the ice cream.

My Academy jeans don't fit anymore, though twenty years from now
I'll go on OA and lose the weight — I'll wear those jeans when I'm 88.
Back then, though, the Sloan wives were giving two parties per week
with all the deviled eggs and pigs-in-a-blanket you could eat

with your martinis, each wife trying to outdo the other with her pies
and sweets. Linda will be like that — she'll make some man
a loyal wife, and John will be as good a provider as a Scout. Sharon
can't seem to get with the program, though, using John's microscope.

She's always wanted to use his things. Back in Key West
she asked for a Lionel train like John's — as if there were trains
for girls. Ree got her a wind-up Toonerville Trolley
but we could see she was disappointed. It wiggled and tooted

across the floor — she called it a train puppy. For her birthday
she wanted an Erector set since John wouldn't let her play with his.
She thought it was a toy. Ree got her a baking set with real cake mix,
little pans and spoons. We thought she'd like kitchen tools but she didn't.

In fairness, the counselor at school said she scored off the charts
on mechanical ability — spotting the direction of moving gears —
but she's lousy in math. How could she be an engineer when she cries
over the nine-times-table? Well, she'll forget all about it

when the hormones kick in. For now we let her sneak John's things
when he isn't looking as long as she puts everything back
where it belongs. Right now she's making slides of water drops
from puddles in the yard, searching for other worlds.

Stay Awake
February 13, 1959

I have a terrible time staying awake,
even with the pills I take.

On this last book, the text was so difficult,
I had to read most of it out loud in order to keep awake.

The Autobiography of Lincoln Steffens was really good
but Systems Engineering was a killer. It's a book I should
have liked, but it stalled in my brain like a rusty gear
— and I'm supposed to be a systems engineer!

The book I like the best of all the works assigned
is The Scarlet Letter by Nathaniel Hawthorne, about a man who pined
for a married woman (this takes place in Puritan days)
and he's a bachelor minister — but no matter how hard he prays

he still wants her and she wants him because they really love each other
and her husband is this sneaking old man who leaves her
alone a lot and — well, you know how it goes. There weren't enough
girls to go around in a little village, so it was really rough

on bachelors. So what were they supposed to do? Well, the upshot is they
get pregnant and she's called before the elders to confess, but she won't say
who did it — while he keeps quiet since he's the only minister they've got.
So she's banished to the forest with her little girl to live alone. The plot

is about the good of the community versus individual needs, but I think
about my girls and I wonder if it's right that one person's life should shrink
away like that while the man goes free. Hawthorne thinks it's wrong —
in the end Dimmsdale, the pastor, dies from guilt because he can't belong

to a community he's betrayed. I asked Ree would it be better if Dimmesdale came
clean? and she said What kind of minister would let a woman take all the blame?
He was a plain coward to her way of thinking. I can see her point, of course,
but she's never been a man on a ship in the middle of the ocean, with every source

of love or pillow talk or even tender eyes a thousand miles away.
Any sailor knows why Dimmesdale paid the price he had to pay.

A Point of View

February 18, 1959

Ree is out to her bridge this evening. She was at a bridge
lunch at the faculty club yesterday too.
My heavens we play bridge a lot — and Ree plays
twice as often as I do. These social rounds are hard
for her, with executives' wives used to the high life
and very well dressed. At least my blue collar
got ironed out at Annapolis — Ree's been reinventing
herself on her own. She's spent more on clothes
this year than ever — it helps that she's got a great figure.

Mrs. Allen was in this morning for a visit —
the mother of one of Linda's friends.
Not nearly as stylish as Ree, somewhat portly,
a regular housewife — but a nice lady.
Linda had a school dance today.
She is taking notice of boys, though boys
lag behind in the noticing business.
Still, Linda's a blonde, developing a figure.
She is more than enthusiastic about
dancing these days.

On the other hand, *Sharon had her girl scouts today*
as usual, and we have signed her permission slip
for the trip to Peterborough. They are going to learn
how to tap maple trees for the syrup. Not much
call for that these days, but good for her to be outside
anyway. *It is a Boston College summer camp*
that BC allows the schools to use during the winter.
We got her the new style of "ski-pajamas"
to sleep in a bunk house, and fitted her out
with John's waterproof boots to weather the snow.
The girls do not take any dresses or skirts
so I guess they rough it.

THE KIDS
March 4, 1959

Tomorrow the children start back to school
after their weeks vacation — much to our pleasure.
We love them, of course, but all three
are annoying these days and on top of that Ree
was elected chairwoman of the Sloan Wives' Club —
a big honor, but lots of work. Honestly,
a military wife should know better
than to volunteer.

The week was just about the end of Ree.
And even though school is in session again
The tension continues to build up
as the year comes toward its end
what with Linda emoting over how Ree cut her bangs,
and how her fruit flies died right before the Science Fair.

Sharon trails around in a daze with <u>Bullfinch's Mythology</u>
in one hand and <u>Winnie the Pooh</u> in the other
while John just mopes in his room — doesn't take the trash out,
won't answer when spoken to, and even then retorts
under his breath — at least Ree thinks so —
and the children feel it and are reacting
by not doing the things they should,
chiefly homework. Honestly, what else do they have to do?

Dad, remember how I did mine every day? Why, studying
was my third favorite thing after stamps and football —
my first chore after serving the paper and collecting dues.
I was motivated to get into Maryland, or even the Academy,
even then, but John doesn't seem to care about the Navy.
He needs a job in my opinion, but Ree says no,
he has to study. She saves all her quarters
at the end of each day
to put in John's college jar.

Beer and Basketball
March 4, 1959

John got hit by a basketball yesterday
and I had to get him new
frames for his glasses — charcoal gray
for $9. What with his doctor bill for five dollars
and exray for ten, basketball is an expensive game.
Well, we can be grateful that he didn't get injured,
get glass in his eye, but after the October hayride
when he got kicked in the face
and we had to replace his glasses the first time,
I wonder if it's just John being difficult.
He feels sorry, though — we can see that.
We are glad he has been able to take part
in a sport this year so it is well worth it.

Sharon got to her overnight visit with Carol
and to the Ice Follies. Linda had two more babysitting jobs.
Ree and I were out to parties both Friday and Saturday this week,
one by the operations exec from Campbell's Soup
on Friday night and the Terrys on Saturday —
Ed's a finance manager at DuPont.
Ree likes Liz Terry because she's not stuffy.
The pace is getting fast again in that respect. These corporate men
have big budgets for entertainment, not like us government fellows.
Federal rules are so strict about bribery that we can't spend
more than fifty dollars a quarter. Ree feels embarrassed
that all she can serve is deviled eggs and Swedish meat balls
when the other wives serve big trays of cold cuts and canapés
and champagne.
I tell her we get as high on beer as on bubbly,
but it's no comfort to her.

CHEER UP
March 4, 1959

It's a blessing in disguise that you are home these days
when Grandaddy needs someone to cheer him up.
He was always so active it must be frustrating to sit around.
I wonder if he walks his old post office route in his mind?
He knows Foggy Bottom like his own face,
though with the boat house torn down for the tidal basin
it hardly looks like the same town we were born in.
The whole neighborhood is gone
what with the Kennedy Center going up.
I had not realized that he had anything so serious as a blood clot,
but I guess there are all degrees of seriousness in such a thing.
No good acting like it's a catastrophe
when everyone is just trying to get through to the next day
and mother could have another breakdown
what with everyone getting old and ill.
Grandaddy, it seems to me, tends to be pessimistic about his health —
you know how I always remind him of how he used to tell me
it would probably be his last visit way back in my first year at Annapolis,
nearly twenty years ago.
It runs in the family. Fast-forward sixty years — Sharon's been telling me good-bye
since I turned eighty and now I'm ninety-four.

When I lived in Bloomington to be near Linda at the U,
Sharon would come visit from Seattle — she liked Ruth Anne
a lot. Third-time wife's a charmer. But when I took her to the bus station
or the airport, Sharon always puddled up
like she would never see me again.
Now that I'm bed-ridden and addle-pated in Seattle
with nothing to die of in this bubble of custodial care,
she wonders if she'll ever see the last of me.
At least she got around to getting married.
She and Jim come by to chat and cheer me up, play hymns
on the tablet — "Rock of Ages," "A Mighty Fortress," and the Navy hymn,
eternal father strong to save whose arm doth bind the restless wave
my favorite. They also play <u>The Washington Post March</u>.
Dad, there's no place like the first home,
waiting for the last.

PLUMBER
March 6, 1959

*Another thing that has sabotaged me this week
is a bathroom faucet.* Let's face it, my thesis is hard
what with research, writing, fighting fear — I'm thirty-eight,
and I ain't what I used to be — so I goof off. I read TIME,
I work around the house, I try to make Ree happy.
Anything but study.

*It was more than a simple washer that was causing the leak,
but I had to do a lot of work and make a trip downtown
before I found it out.* I might have found the washer I needed
closer to home, but I wanted to go somewhere —
anywhere but Newton Centre. Just for half an hour
I wanted to engineer something, just fix something
like on the Mulaney, without a kid whining or a wife scolding
or a book accusing me of neglect. Or thesis making me feel
like an idiot.

*I even had to overhaul the cutoff valve in the basement which evidently
had not been used in many years.* The old lady who rents this place
makes sure the wallpaper — shepherds playing Pan-pipes
and Little-Bo-Peeps — isn't peeling off, and that Ree
has cake platters of every size. But cutoff valves?
The basement is dark and damp, no place for an old lady.
So I oiled it, I cranked the nut, worked graphite into the joints.
In the end I still had to call the plumber.

SKID ROW

March 6, 1959

One thing the faucet trouble did for me in spite of the bad feature,
was to send me on a trip down into Boston's South Side.
I didn't really send myself — the faucet sent me —
which OK'd my little furlough.

It is the Skid Row here — but it is not too terribly run down. You'd expect worse
what with the factories moving to suburbia and men left jobless
in the old town — moms waiting tables, addressing envelopes,
kids serving papers to make ends meet.

The thing that I enjoyed was stopping at a men's bar there —
like being back at the Academy, without
the complication of women, or on a ship
where you understand silence
or why you're fighting.
You can laugh at a dirty joke.

There were a number of old men — half of the population there
is single men over sixty —
(I laugh to remember when sixty seemed old — I, who lived
through three wives and died at ninety-five.)

— and it was a real old fashioned bar with wooden stools and TV
and eight different kinds of draught beer, ale, and stout.
Which is why a man can relax at a bar
like nowhere else. Did God make dives
to compensate us for making the world go round?
Ree has bridge club, after all,
and garden club.
As much as I love her,
it's better here,
just for a little minute.

I had a glass of ale, a huge liverwurst sandwitch
with a side dish of pickled beets and onions for 30 cents.
Now I wish I had tried the stout,
although I am told I would not like it.
Who told me that? Was it you? I wish you'd been on the stool
beside me, Dad — you on one side, Grandaddy
on the other. You get old watching the contrails
of the ones you love. They start to disappear
while you still stare into the sky.
But my, that liverwurst was good.

March 8, 1959

A funny thing Happened Saturday while the family
was out shopping
and I was home studying.
I was reading <u>Our Man in Havana</u> when
A little girl called who was babysitting
over in Needham.
We don't know her — she just dialed a random number.
This was back when you could do that — so few numbers,
and most people with phones were middle class folks
with bedside tables, gossip benches, extensions in the kitchen.

She couldn't contact the baby's mother
and her own mother was out,
so she Just called a number
to ask for advice.
She sounded like a baby herself — high-pitched little voice,
like a cup full of tears,
fearful she had done something terrible.

I told her not to make the baby eat the spinach
and to just give her the bottle
and put her to bed,
I could see the baby's face in my mind,
screwed up like vinegar — Johnny
and Linda and Sherry all the same —
they hated spinach, though oddly
they all like it now

but not to worry because nothing was wrong.
Babies are like rubber — they bounce right up
unless something deliberate happens —
like those bad parents who beat their children.
During the Depression
it was more common.

She called back a little later to say
that the baby went right to sleep.
I congratulated her, said she was a big girl
a good sitter, the mother would never know.

I have not had a problem like that for years.
Thank god.
Now to bed.

Ree at Piney Point
Summer 1960

REE
April 10, 1959

Ree has gone with a couple of other
girls up to a woolen mill today. I think
they had just gone shopping rather
than from any great interest
in the textile industry. She'll come back
with something pretty — she always
does, then she models it for me,
twirling her skirts in the living room.

I always liked that about Ree — how
she looks great in her clothes, never without
lipstick and Shalimar, her waist just right
for my arm. The Waves looked good
in their uniforms — we saluted their
legs as much as their rank, and their cute
curls under those jaunty caps, with those
close-fitting jackets — but girls dressed like girls

is what turns my engine over. Even
as kids, when I had to baby-sit Ree
on Newton Street and drag her along
to the movies she wore her dungarees
just so, her sweater neat, hair
braided and shiny — I noticed her
even then, a real girl, hard to please,
serious. Only when I sat on the sofa

and read the <u>Saturday Evening Post</u> aloud
so her mom could practice shorthand up to speed
(she got hired at the War Department)
did Ree start being nice to me. That was twenty-
five years ago. She was twelve. I was thirteen.
…I took her down to Derben Park
restaurant in the market last night
and she had a huge roast beef,

still slim as a girl. She wore her new Pendleton
jacket — blue plaid — and chattered on about
power looms, shuttles, Jacquard heads,
and two thousand weft insertions per minute.

DISCIPLINES
April 10, 1959

This will be a very short letter.
I do not even have
the writter up on the desk.

Shenever I just have a few
lines to type I leave it
down here on the coffee

table and squat down to type.
This way I am not tempted
to go on and on because my legs

get tired. My life is full of
these clever disciplines.
I place my daily task list

under my coffee cup
so I won't relax too much.
I set the timer on the stove

when I'm reading — its squall
is the best interrupter.
I empty my change

into the brass pot every night —
the kids sneak quarters.
Ree wishes I wasn't so

rigid, but they'd be sorry
if I stopped — *Now I must*
finally get to that extra chapter.

Legs tired — love to Mother.

Jack and Cumbie
Key West, Flordia, 1958

SMOKING
April 22, 1959

I guess it is a bad habit,
but I have taken to smoking
these little cigars that they make
on the cigarette machines, I still smoke
my pipes, too, so this little den
is full of smoke most of the time.
They are probably too little
for you, these cigarillos, though you

are smaller than you used to be. Funny
how children think dads
are gigantic, then grow to tower
over stooped old men
with crabbed hands and pot
bellies whose pee, heard
through the bathroom door,
is an intermittent trickle

instead of the Niagara
of school day mornings
waiting my turn. Now my den
is full of smoke just when
you can't smoke anymore, run
a mile, turn a summersault.
And *sex* — impossible — old mother
in her wrapper, whining, cold.

Suddenly I shove papers
aside, bound down to the kitchen,
ambush Ree making chicken a la king,
roll her onto the sofa! Kids at school,
Another World mutters on the radio,
Ree's floury hands pattern my chest
until smoke drives us shrieking,
naked to the oven, grabbing

her forgotten muffins. We're wrapped
in skin and surprise, sitting side-
by-side, nibbling on blackened blueberries
in the breakfast nook.

Cape Cod
April 24, 1959

Much to our surprise we got a letter
from Sharon this morning. She is probably
the only ten (no, eleven) year old alive

who would think to write a letter home
on a three (no, five) day trip to Cape Cod
with those Jewish department store folks —

the Lazaruses. Their daughter is Sharon's
pal, poor kid. Imagine having the name
of a moldering dead man — like a mummy!

Well, Jesus loved Lazarus — like Sharon, who loves
anyone who loves her back. She hardly knows
what a Jew is — heck, she barely knows they're rich,

merely saying they have a <u>Saturday Evening Post</u>
cover in the sun room — an orginal Norman Rockwell!
Or mentioning at her girlfriend's birthday

they wore costumes like lords and ladies, rode ponies
around the back yard. And now Cape Cod.
The letter said fairly little — a shingled cottage,

sand dunes, drift wood, a yellow moon. The fact
of the letter was curious — that she thought
of us just when we'd stopped thinking of her

for a little while. Sharon is cute, like a shy dog,
ready to be petted by rich or poor, gentile or Jew.
She'll come back soon. We ought to miss her more.

Sloan Reunion
May 2, 1959

This has been a busy week for us
because it was the week of the Sloan Reunion —
all these smart guys coming back from Northrop Grumman, Raytheon,
General Electric, Safeway, Screen Gems, the Army.

We went to most of the activities because M.I.T. brings in the big guns
to tell you you're the best of everyone, capable of anything —
trying to convince ordinary men that they're more
than the husbands of their wives and the fathers of their children.

On Thursday we had a series of talks during the day while the women
had a fashion show and lunch. Ree said they had shrimp salad in endive leaves,
whatever those are, and finger sandwiches with caviar and cucumber.
She said she felt like the First Lady (though she's a whole lot cuter than Mamie).

Our most interesting talk was by General Gavin. He is the one who resigned in the missile
controversy — opposing Long Range Stand Off weapons — later in the dog house
for refusing suicidal combat orders in Vietnam. He was on the young
side, like us, in 1959 but died at 86 — a four-star general.

We had an evening of cocktails and dinner and a talk by both Sloan
— the founder of the Business School *and Killian* — the president of M.I.T.
We have to get used to these fancy events, Dad — me the son of a Western Union man
and Ree the daughter of a stenographer and itinerant dock worker.

I will be seeing you in three weeks when we come down
for our Washington field trip. I expect we'll meet some senators and congressmen —
maybe even the President — in that big white house where long ago
you delivered the Washington Post to a white-gloved butler.

Tickled to Death

May 4, 1959

We went to M.I.T. night at the Boston Pops last night
and we had a real surprise.
There was a lot of buzz about something special
on the program for the engineers.
I thought it might be the selections,
like the 1812 Overture or Sousa marches.
But guess what, Dad? You won't believe it —

Danny Kaye, who has been a guest conductor with them in the past,
showed up and did some impromptu conducting.
He was just as funny in person as in all those great films —
remember The Short Happy Life of Walter Mitty,
or the time we first saw a Danny Kaye film
at the matinee when I was still at McKinley Tech?
It was a short subject about a Russian aristocrat
being chased by Bolsheviks.

He was a regular riot. First he ran on stage
with a fistful of batons in his hand
and crowded Conductor Dickson right off the podium.
He flailed his arms around so much
he fell off the stage!
Then he climbed back up
and conducted "The Flight of the Bumble Bee"
with a fly swatter.

He is a favorite of Ree's so she was tickled to death.
Maybe I never told you this, but Ree almost died
for real when we went to see The Court Jester —
she laughed so hard about the pellet with the poison
in the vessel with the pestle that she choked on a cough drop.

I enjoyed it immensely too.
It was on the front page of the morning papers.
Blessed relief from the nuclear arms race
or that poor family from Oregon who got kidnapped.
Their daughter's body — the girl Sharon's age —
washed up at the Bonneville Dam.

TEMPORARY REDEMPTION
May 4, 1959

Ree was down to school today for the regular conferences about John.
I would have gone myself but for being too worried
about my own thesis conference.
He has done very well this year after all but I suspect I'm the one
who dropped the ball this term. The Profs don't say so — don't want to admit
they made a mistake admitting me.

The low marks he has gotten were due mostly to the teachers' believing
that he would ease up if they marked too easily.
That's what they suggested to Ree, at any rate, but she's like a terrier
when it comes to John — don't tell her he has faults! She'd probably sink her teeth
into that Latin teacher. (Wish she could do that to my thesis advisor.)

I guess they know best, those high school teachers — better to placate an angry mother
than tell the obvious truth about sullen teens — *but it gave us some unhappy times*
around the house. John was our quarterback, the only boy, the Cumberland Hope.
Of course we had to push him.

A lot of credit goes to him for pulling himself out of his grumpy spell.
Not that it lasted — he dropped out of college, joined the Navy
as a common seaman, for F's sake — even though he tested so highly
they tried to force him into Officers Training School.

*Now I have to stop…*but, oh — all those quarters Ree saved
for John's education, and yet it was the girls,
those unsuspected girls! —
who astonished us with Ph.D.s.

PARTY OF THE YEAR
June 1, 1959

Saturday night we were at the Divols'
for a party. We were raided by the police
for making so much noise singing. We figured
that made it the best party of the year

automatically. We weren't drunk, really,
but Ree had three manhattans after
wine with dinner — I stuck with martinis
all the way and fared better.

We rolled back the carpet, danced
to Benny Goodman and Sinatra
though Ree preferred watching —
one pretty knee folded under,

her gimlet eye stopping me
from dancing with anyone else.
She still accused me when we
got home, though I hushed her,

the kids asleep across the hall. War's
been over fifteen years but still
she sees girls in every port,
opportunity wherever we gather.

The police were good natured —
rather like they wanted to join in.
We offered them a drink and Janie
Divol showed them her garters

just as a joke. Everyone laughed
but Ree. She thinks Janie is cheap
even though her husband is Managing
Director of the turbine unit at G.E.

We collapsed into bed as if shot, but
the morning headaches came like sirens,
flashing lights, and a gang of vets roaring
Show me the way to go home!

Mock Businesses
June 4, 1959

We divided into three mock companies
and made decisions on a simulated market
for our products. Our decisions were fed
into the IBM 650 and then we repeated

the process. We did eight quarters all day.
Now, of course, we could run the calendar
in an hour, or half an hour. Ten minutes
perhaps. I don't know. A millisecond?

We thought it was a miracle then. I spent
my youth with a slide rule, that beautiful
mathematician's tool the young
now gawp at, as though we were either

geniuses or fools. I wore one as a tie clip,
in high school, upside-down so I could tip it
up, use it in class. No one uses them anymore,
or wears ties to school for that matter.

I was an early adopter of computers,
used a Brother, Atari, Lanier machine,
ran torpedo testing on punch cards,
tapes, floppies, media of all kinds.

Things are too fast for me now, though,
or I'm too slow. Annapolis, M.I.T. —
all behind me. I contemplate the cloudy
galaxy — my own disintegrating matter —

knowing I once was an engineer
of some stature. Now, all those
quarters — how many? — four times
eighty-nine, ninety — pixilated, dispersed.

Near End
June 5, 1959

We have nearly come to an end of this series of letters.
Sadly, your letters to me didn't survive —
and Mom such a careful saver. But she was muddled
when she died in Orlando where my last job was.
Naval Training Devices Center, Trident subs.

We fought over Mom. Ree wanted to send
her back to D.C. after you died, Dad,
because her OCD was driving us crazy,
touching every little thing: kids, meals,
housekeeping. Ree hated how Mom rode
in the front seat, like the Blessed Mother.
I was a good son, though — kept her with us
in a little house in the Judsons' backyard
where I could walk over to check in
once a day, bring groceries.

Our mail here has started to fall off
so I assume that some of it has started
to come to Newton Street. The kids spent
that summer at Piney Point while we waited
for news on which job I got — hit the jackpot
with a spot on the NATO team in Rome.
Ree learned Italian, chaperoned the kids'
school trips to Florence, Venice, catacombs.
Imagine that, Dad — from Newton Street
to the Via Veneto!

I spent all day yesterday getting odds and ends
cleared up and I still have a long way to go.
I didn't know then how bad the clutter would get.
The invention of self-storage in the 1970s
would create a Cumberland junk pile that lasted thirty years —
once started, never cleared: moldering albums, baby shoes,
your telegraph, Dad, and mother's Gregg notebooks,
boxes of costume jewelry, buttons, post cards, bundles of letters
tied in string: 1940, 1941,1942, 1943, stamps unsticking, falling
like snowflakes. But my files, Dad — files and files and files — were my own
OCD. I don't know why I got so paranoid about it. Wouldn't let the kids
sort it even though it ended up in their garages anyway.
It turned out OK, though. We still have my letters now
because Sharon found them,
saved them, from the junk pile.

THE LETTERS

CUMBERLAND, USN

BRISTOL (DD 857)
ET POST OFFICE
CISCO, CALIFORNIA

In case of Jack Cumberland
being reported missing or
dead follow instructions of this letter.

Mr. Harold L. Keller
Mound City Trust Co.
St. Louis
Missouri

JUL
17
1945
NAVY

Free

PASSED BY
NAVY CENSOR

To Ree
My Wife

48

6 July 1945

My own Dear Ree:

Although I'll write you more, this is really my last letter to you. We've spent so much of our time in the mail that it seems right that I should tell you goodbye this way. I can't say that I don't like writing this because I have enjoyed every word I have ever written you. I didn't feel the need for this the last time out, but somehow I just feel that this time is it. I think my luck has run out. My faith hasn't though — not by a long shot. It's just that you'll have a long wait here on earth before we're together again. I ask only one thing of you — make it a happy wait. I won't tell you how I think you can make it a happy wait. You're the only one who can know that. I can tell you what I think is the best way — marry again. I mean that sincerely. If you think you've found someone you can be sure of, then go ahead. Don't do it for Johnny or because I suggest it though. Do it because of the same full, rich feelings of body and soul that first brought us together. And don't believe that those feelings in you must die with me. I have known your love and I know how great and capable it is. I have your love—all in all—and I'll never have to share it. If the things you've felt for me are ever felt again after I've gone, they'll be felt for me. Through God we are always together. If ever you can love again, you'll find me there. Anyone that you could love would have me in him. I'll always love you, and in God's time we'll be together. I've often wondered how it would work out in heaven if you married again. I know now. There would be three of us and I would have the one fast and true friend I've always lacked here on earth. So things are never as bad as they seem at first. You're so very young and so very beautiful that life has got to give you the joy and happiness you've always taken from it. And one more thing about this marriage. (I would like to be the best man.) Don't foul it up by thinking your second love can't be as strong as the first. Get all the way into it—that's the only way it can work. If you're sure enough to take the step, then everything there was between us is an open book to someone else for the first time. That's the way I want it — but be sure. But enough of that. From all the words I've put into it, you'd think I were trying to get you married off before you were out of the black — that I hope you never got into. I'd be just as happy myself if you could sputter along happily through life with only me watching over you from up here. Knowing me the way you do you'll realize that I couldn't seriously consider the possibility of anyone of my calibre existing on earth after I've left the old place. as much as I long to live and as much as I long for you, I don't feel at all bad about leaving. I pray every night and many times a day that we may be together safely after the war. But I feel that I am leaving and I look forward to it with all the eagerness and excitement I felt before I left for the academy. I'll just go ahead and wait for you. Maybe you'll visit me in a dream sometime before you come for good. Dearest Kee, yours is the hard part. But I don't feel sorry for you. after the crushing hurt and hopeless loneliness has been mellowed by time, there'll be many, many things to bring you joy. I won't mention them because they are too numerous, but stop and think when you read this, and don't forget they're there. And never regret, for my account, that I left so early. The brightest lives were the shortest. I've had one prayer that I built when I was young and have never denied through all the changes life has brought me through

> To have a full, rich life,
> And live it to the core;
> Then die in the line of duty —
> I ask for nothing more.

My life has had everything that a man could ask. If our love were the only thing in it, it would have been full and rich. But I've had more, and all of it I've enjoyed. Each memory is a blessing and it would take another lifetime to count them all. But the sweetest of them are the memories of you and us. You are my whole life and always will be. I can't say more than that. I won't go back over what we've meant to one another and done to one another. That would only hurt me now and you later. I've written many more letters that were longer and better than this, but I've said what I wanted to and that's what I set out to do. The things I haven't said are the most important, and those are the things I want you to know. Time is but an empty wall between us, and in His time we'll be together as we have always been and shall ever be.

I love you,

Jack

Jack Cumberland
Class of 1944
United States Naval Academy
Annapolis, Maryland

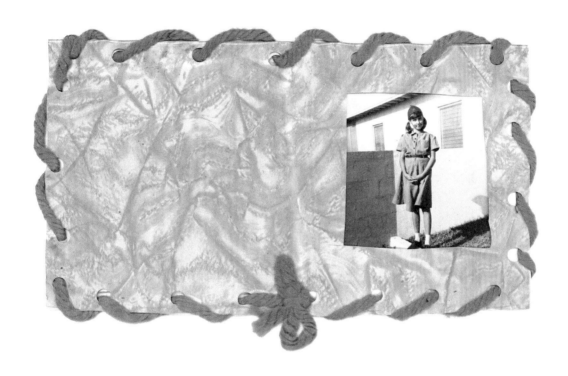

Sharon Cumberland
Key West, Florida
May 1958

Sharon Lee Cumberland

Mr. Richard L. Goldupp
Piney Point, Maryland

PINEY POINT
JUN
18
1958
MD.

Mr. and Mrs. John Cumberland
9 Whittlesey Road
Newton Centre Mass.

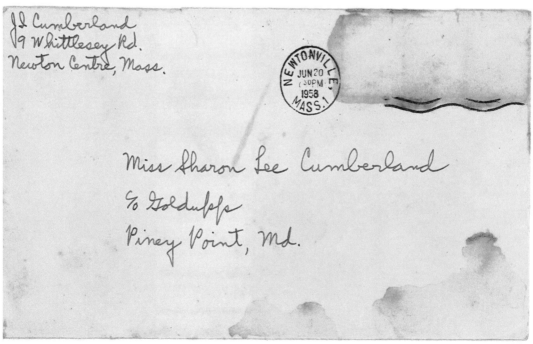

J. Cumberland
9 Whittlesey Rd.
Newton Centre, Mass.

NEWTONVILLE
JUN 20
30 PM
1958
MASS. 1

Miss Sharon Lee Cumberland
℅ Goldupp
Piney Point, Md.

Dear Mom and Dad,
    How do you like
our new home? Hope yo
like it. I know I will.
    How does Elmer like
it? I hope he likes it
too.
    I miss you but not
for long becaus I'll be
with you soon. Is it
snowing? I hope so.
I'm going to have to
do some work on my
sled.   (over)

because of my toothpast
stripe. I love to see the
stripes. I brush my teeth
with it cause it also
tastes like peperment. You
should get some. It's good.
    I hope there is
lots of kids to play
with up there in Boston.
    Are we going on
the train or with
Gramp and Grama?

I can't hardly wait to
be up there.
    We can't go to
Grandma Opal's on the
bus caus it costs to much
We have to go in the
car. But we will have
fun there.
    You don't have
to worry about me
brushing my teeth

Dad, you forgot your
barset. Should we bring
it with us?

                Love
                Sharon

            Ⓧ Ⓧ

P.S. I'm sorry if my
writing is bad.

Friday June 20, 1958

Dear Sharon,

Mother and I were very pleased to get your letter today. We miss you very much and getting a letter from you is the next best thing to talking to you.

We like our new home very much. Mother is in love with it because it is roomy and furnished in very good taste. Elmer likes it because he has a lot of room to run around in. He also likes the outdoors with the trees and bushes to climb and hide in.

No, it is not snowing. It only snows in the winter time and we have all of summer and fall ahead of us before you will see snow. The grass and trees are green now and we have beautiful roses in our yard. All the trees will lose their leaves before snow comes.

I saw some Stripe Toothpaste in the store yesterday and thought about you as soon as I saw it. I pointed it out to Mother and we agreed that we didn't need to worry about your tooth brushing.

You will be coming up with your grandparents

when you come. If Grandpa Richard doesn't want to make the trip, Grandpa Cumbie will drive you up.

We thought about my bar set while we were unpacking our bar things and we remembered that we had forgotten it. Yes, you should bring it with you when you come. Thank you.

There was a letter from the school waiting for us when we got here. You will be in Oak Hill Elementary School. However, the school is so crowded that your grade, the sixth, will be housed in the Meadowbrook Junior High School. It is a brand new shool just next door to the elementary school. John and Linda will be there too. It is a short walk from home.

The nearest stores are 1.7 miles away and you will have to be very careful going there on your bike. But there are all kinds of stores as well as the library and chuch all together in the same town area of Newton Centre.

Mother and I look forward to hearing from you again soon. Tell Grandma we got her letter too.

Love,
Dad
xxx ooo

9 Whittlesey Road
Newton Centre, Mass.

December 6, 1958

Dear Friends,

Are you surprised to receive our Christmas letter to you from the Greater Boston Area? This year we are a Sloan Fellow at M.I.T. By that piece of bad grammar we mean to explain that the fellowship is a family undertaking. Not only did Ree take part in the application and final interview, but she is attending a sample of classes.

There are thirty-seven of us sent here by our companies as complete families, the men to study industrial management for twelve months. Jack's "company" is the Navy Department, of course.

This year we are departing from our usual practice of mailing as close to Christmas as possible and sending you this early in Advent. WE WANT YOU TO HAVE OUR ADDRESS HERE ON WHITTLESEY ROAD SO THAT WE WILL NOT MISS HEARING FROM YOU THIS YEAR!

And now the details. Even though the year began in Key West, it hardly seems like it because all our thoughts were on the trip to Boston. Even when our Christmas letter was written last year we were in successive stages of selection. When the award came on April First, and we had convinced ourselves that it was not an April Fool's joke, we started preparations to leave. Then, on the Fourth of June we started up the Keys hauling the largest Nation-Wide rented trailer available with the World's most tightly packed stationwagon. After a short rest at Piney Point, Maryland, where we left the children for a half summer with their Grandparents, we proceded to take up residence in our lovely house here in the suburbs of Boston. It is completely furnished (in a quaint way) just to Ree's taste. Jack's study just holds him and his desk and we all take turns braving the clouds of pipe smoke that pour out when we pass his coffee in to him.

Returning to school after fifteen years was a shock to Jack, naturally. But in the Sloan Program M.I.T. has contrived to make it a group suffering. In addition to regular class work, he is currently working on four of the six term papers for this term as well as his thesis. Waiting to get into the typewriter is a writeup on the President of the stock exchange-- Jack's contribution to the preparation for the New York field trip next week.

Ree will journey to New York to help wind up the week there, and we will see "Bells Are Ringing". We were nearly first nighters when we saw "Flower Drum Song" on its third night here in Boston on its pre-Broadway shake-down.

If she survives, Ree will have had quite a year. While the men study, the women run the families, attend concerts, plays and the like, and sharpen up their Bridge to the point of unfair advantage.

The children have held up well in the highly progressive and competitive Newton School System. John and Linda in the Ninth and Eighth grades are taking the experimental Illinois Algebra. John's paper on "The Printed Word" had Father speculating as to whether M.I.T. might accept it as his master's thesis. All three children are in Cotillion this year. They simply take up where the Sloan children in this house left off last year, with ready-made friends and activities. Sharon can hardly wait to put the sleds back into service since she hasn't had an opportunity to wear the paint off the runners of the sled she got four Christmases ago in Maryland. The children's growth is especially impressive when we see them in their new winter wardrobes. In fact, we wish we could see them more in their own and less in Mother's and Father's. John's inroads are still limited to bow ties and stretch socks, but the girls are an inch above and an inch below their mother and they seem to consider anything from sweaters to skirts fair game.

And now the pet paragraph. We almost left it out this year because of the necessity of recalling the passing of Pocahontas in her sixteenth year. Also the kitten Mathilda turned out to be part wildcat, and after sending Ree to the doctor for a tetanus shot, was exchanged at the animal shelter for a big yellow tiger cat named Elmer. Elmer is close to perfection in the feline trade and after ten months, we are still waithing to see what his one fault will be.

This is an exciting year for us and we could write on about it for longer than you would care to read. But this much will tell you where we are and what we are doing. We look forward to hearing from all of you this Christmas and hope you will let us know what you are doing. The Sappenfield, Culjat, and Morgan letters finally persuaded us that the Christmas letter is the finest way to make friendships live, and in this, our third letter, we would like to encourage more of you to join us in this annual undertaking--if not this year, then next.

We wish you a Merry Twelve Days of Christmas and three hundred and sixty-five days in a Happy New Year.

                                THE CUMBERLANDS
                                    Jack
                                    JACK
                                    Ree
                                    REE
                                    John
                                    JOHN
                                    Linda
                                    LINDA
                                    Sharon
                                    SHARON

Monday Evening
January 5, 1959

Dear Dad,

    While I have the typwritter out to get a letter off to G.E.
about some marketing information I have been asking them for
I will just run off a quick letter to you. I find that I type
faster than I write these days so it is easy for me to get
onto paper this way. I do it all the time in connection with
my thesis conferences. After I talk to someone I get it down
on paper right away or I forget it. I even took an exam with
the typewriter last night after I got that postcard off to you
and Mom. It was a take-home exam in labor relations — if you
can imagine such a thing as a take-home exam. I was to allow
myself two hours and not to look anything up after I started.
This year is different from any other year of schooling I have
had in many ways.
    We got a large bundle of mail today but it was mostly my
Wall Street Journals and magazines. Mother's card was in the
bundle though. She must have sent it the minute we got out of
the house.
    [...]
    It is very cold here with a strong wind blowing. The
policeman on Sharon's patrol post lets her warm up in his car
and even drove her home both times today. Ree just left for
her weekly bridge with the wives. Now I had better get back to
my studies. Remember me to Frank if you are still down there
with him. You could not have had a better roommate.
                                My love to you and Mom,
                                Jack

Wednesday Morning
January 7, 1959

[handwritten]

Dear Dad,

    It's a darn shame you had to go back for more work by Dr. Sterling on the very day we hoped you would go home. Ree called Mom last night because it was my dinner seminar night and I couldn't get free to call. It was good to know you are getting along fine and lost so little blood.

    Ree and I are more happy than we can say about your return to the Church. We were happy to hear that Frank did too. That priest must feel like he hit the jackpot in your room.

    Wednesday is our one full day of classes so I am leaving like a regular office worker and must go now.

Love,
Jack

Dear Dad,

No news about you in this morning's mail so I will get
this letter off now anyway. I am skipping my only class today
since the marketing course is of little interest to me and the
instructor is very poor. I have more important work to do here
at home. Ree will mail my letter for me on her way to take
Sharon to dancing this afternoon.

You will have to excuse the way I write these letters to
you because I give practically no thought to how I am writing —
I just let my thoughts run out through my fingers as they come.
With my tight time schedule this permits me to get something in
the mail to you each day without consuming much of my time at
all. I know you are glad to hear from me and I know your days
must be terribly long. I just cannot be thankful enough for
Frank being there with you. I know I enjoyed so much talking
with him when I was there. I enjoyed my visits with you no end
— especially the late evenings when the hospital was so quiet.
The whole world seems to be noisy these days. Looking back on
my trip down I think the visits with you and Frank did me more
good than they did you or Frank. Now that I am back to the
study grind, I find that my battery has been recharged.

Now isn't this just my luck. I just got a call from the
marketing instructor's secretary that there is to be a special
lecture by an outside speaker at one this afternoon so that I
will have to go in after all. That's life. It will at least be
interesting.

I am smoking my new mearsham pipe that Ree gave me for
Christmas. It is a real joy. The most surprising thing about
it is the amber bit. The amber bit gives the thing an entirely
different taste. I hear people say that but it is still a
surprise.

Last night Ree and I just couldn't keep from playing hookey
and running down to see "Inn of the Sixth Happiness". It was
well worth the stolen time, too. After the morning lecture on
international economics in which we discussed tarriffs, I was
convinced that there was not a single unselfish person in the
world, but the gal in that story certainly was.

Now I have to go and get dressed for my lecture. We are
all thinking of you all the time and doing our best to pray
you out of the hospital (Frank too, tell him). Joe Choate, my
Roman Catholic car pool mate, the one with the seven children,
was almost as happy as Ree and I to hear about you and Frank
getting back in the fold. He is off to Tarrytown today to get
his New York tags. I am getting my Florida tags by mail through
joe Allen in Key West. More tomorrow.

All of our love,
Jack

Thursday Morning
January 15, 1959

[postcard]

Dear Dad,

It just occurred to me that you may not get the card I
wrote yesterday because I forgot to put the extra stamp on it.
I also remembered that I forgot to stop by Red Cross to pay
back the pint of blood we owe them. I have not given any since
leaving Maryland because there is no bank in Key West, so I am
long overdue anyway. I can do it when I go down to the Bureau
on my D.C. tri[p. We got Mother's airmail letter yesterday
and a card today, both reporting good progress — fine. Now
that things have gotten down to a routine convalescence ther
is no need for Mother to write every day unless she feels so
inclined. I am in an increasingly hectic period of preparation
for my trip plus three end-of-term papers which are due next
week. This short card or note takes practically no time at
all,however,;so it will probably continue. We continue well in
all respects and all send our love, Jack

```
                                        Sunday Evening
                                        February 1, 1959
Dear Folks,
```

Here I am back again to my study and my typewriter. It feels good to be typing rather than writing with my pencil. My thumb is still numb from all the note taking I did on the trip. From now on most of my writing will be on the typewriter again.

I had a fine trip back to Boston. The weather was clear and the ride was smooth and quick, We were in five minutes early so that Ree and the kids did not have to wait at all. We drove right home and had a lazy evening. Ree did not feel very well and then I noticed she had a red rash on her face and neck. It got worse and all the other symptoms of three day measles came along with it. The rash is gone today but she still feels a little bad. The kids think it is very funny. The incubation period, according to Ree's medical encyclopedia, is from ten to fourteen days; so they may not think it is quite so funny in a week or two.

Ree, of course, stayed in bed for awhile this morning while the kids and I went to 9:30 service. But she felt well enough to cook dinner for us. The children had a dress rehearsal for the coronation ceremony of their Gallahad (John) and Fleur de Leis (Girls) Societies — an annual ceremony which takes place next Thursday at church. I took time off to watch Omnibus (Young Abe Lincoln) and to chauffer the kids; so I have not got a lot done today. It was not so much the time out I took, but the odds and ends that had to be taken care of after a week. The mail was the biggest thing. The radiator was no problem at all. The air valve was simply a press fit into the radiator, and it had blown out. It is something that happens in time to all of the valves in the house and there was a replacement valve in the table drawer by my bed. It had self tapping threads and I had it on in less than two minutes with no tools at all.

[...]

That is about all there is to report from here. I have got to get all of my papers from 1st term put away and then get my papers from the trip in order. All that still has to be done before I can start on the actual thesis work. I also understand some of the fellows have gotten some of next term's books and are started on them. I will have to keep at it so I can get a little ahead. That always makes you feel better.

I certainly enjoyed my visit with you. It was especially
good to get out to see Grandad and to get to see Henry while
I was there. The tough dinners are always a treat — I finished
the last of it as a snack this afternoon. Linda was the only
one here who would even take a taste.

We all send our love,
Jack

Dear Dad,

    We are having another beautiful day here again. I only got
out to get a haircut, but it was nice. I figured I had better
get my hair cut since I am going to have to go out into the
world again Saturday night when we are going to a party. This
week of studying at home is closer to a vacation than anything
else I have ever done. I have to keep busy, but you have to
keep busy on a vacation too. The difference between working
on my thesis and just readin or doing other things is not too
great. I guess being at home is the big thing.
    Sharon is at home today too. She seems to have the same
kind of upset that kept Linda and John home also at different
times during the few weeks past. She will be alright by Monday,
or by Sunday, I am sure.
    Our oil burner went on the blink last night. It is the
landlady's responsibility so we have a new controller and a new
thermostat at her expense. Aside from taxes that is the first
she has had since we have been here so that is not too bad.
    Today is report card day for the whole family. I got all
B's just as I expected. We have to get B's to get our degree,
so they are just about in the category of courtesy marks. There
were undoubtedly some A's but it does not mean much.
    John got a poor report for him. One of his marks is an
incomplete that he will have to make up. He also got a C in
Latin, which is greatly below his capabilities. This is not a
good year for him and I am looking forward to getting settled
where he can get a firmer start. Linda is not home with hers yet
and Sharon will have to wait until next week.
    We got a card from Mother today postmarked Wednesday
evening so it seems that the mail does not take long even by
train. Our mailman here is no great shakes, because we get our
TIME a day late almost all of the time. We did every bit as
well in Key West.
    You would think I would have more to writ about abut I
guess that is all I think of right now. I had better get back
to work.

                                        Love,
                                        Jack

```
                                      Sunday Afternoon
                                      February 8, 1959
Dear Dad,

     I have just missed this afternoon's mail so I will not be
mailing this to you until tomorrow morning at school. I have
not been feeling too well today and neither has Ree. We went
to our last party before Lent and we ate and drank too much. I
have been overeating most of the time even without a party, and
then that is usually enough to overdo it. We got to church in
fine shape though and we had a big pork and sourkraut dinner, so
it could not be too bad. I have also gotten a couple of hours
in on my thesis work. But I am afraid I still have more than
half of my interview notes to type up. Now my regular cours
work has started again and I will really have to get going.
     Ree went over to Shopper's World yesterday and got a couple
of ne dresses. They are winter-spring dresses, so all signs are
pointing toward spring. Our weather is spring-like too, even
though we were having a snow flurry on the way to church this
morning.
     Mother's letter came in Saturday's mail. It was especially
newsy. I guess the best news was about your driving again. That
will make a big difference. Being mobile allows you to do more
things. You will be able to get out to see Grandaddy during
the day, which will be wonderful for him since the rest of
the family can only make it in the evenings. It is especially
fortunate that you are able to do that during the first little
while he is out there.
     [...]
     That mixture you have to drink is an unusual one. But it
really is not too far from an eggnog; in fact, I guess that is
what it is. The gellatin is the only non-standard addition. I
would think a little sugar and a dash of nutmeg would make it a
real drink. I am almost tempted to try one myself.
     We were watching that Pat Boone-Dinah Shore show that
Mother mentioned also. Watching television on the networks is a
lot like looking at the moon — you know people miles away are
doing the same thing. I am afraid we did not see the wrastling
The only wrastling I ever watch is when I am with you.
     [...]
```

Sharon has recovered completely from her upset. She went to church with us this morning. We have been blessed with very good health this year. Once the children get out of the young and sickly age it is a lot easier. John is feeling punk because of being homesick for Key West. He heard the Newton High band Friday and they are not as good as the Key West High. Anyway, it made him wish he were back. Ree told him he is just going to have to look ahead rather than back because we definitely will not be going back there. I think it will be a lot better when we have more definite plans. But then when we think about it we realize our plans are pretty darn definite. We will pack up during the week before graduation and we hope to start driving Saturday morning. We will unload the trailer in your garage and leave the kids at Piney Point while Ree and I house hunt. I will plan to take enough time off to spend a good portion of my daytime looking around. This will be the first time I will be able to take my time at it — I hope. Ree and I are looking forward to it. The housing market should be just about right. There is a lot of new construction out in Maryland just now, isn't there? We do not want a new house, but one of those big, old ones in College Park. The new construction is a help to us since it drives the price of older houses down.

Now I just have to get back to work. I get interested in doing other things and I just do not get enough time spent on the thesis. This letter only takes a few minutes, but when I start writing about next spring's plans, I start to sit here and daydream.

[...]

Love,
Jack

                              Monday
                              February 9, 1959
Dear Dad,

    It is a cold and wintry evening here in Boston. The snow is
falling outside, although it should not be because the forecast
did not call for it. It started this afternoon and is still
going strong. But it is not likely to continue since warmer
weather is predicted for tomorrow.

    Today was the first day of our new term and we had two
classes. One class was with Professor Schell, who is the father
of the Sloan program — having persuaded Mr. Sloan to sponsor
it some years ago. He is a professor emeritous, which means
which means he is retired. He puts in as much teaching time as
many of the others however. His subject is executive behavior,
so far as I can determine it. Many of our courses are hard to
identify by the title. Everyone seems to have an idea or two
about how to run a business and they all tell it to us in their
own way.

    The other class we had today was with Elting Morrison,
who is also the chairman of my thesis committee. He teaches a
course in which he endeavors to teach us something about the
American scene. He does this by assigning us one book per week
to read and then letting us talk about it. The first book is the
Autobiography of Benjamin Franklin. I read it as a child and
remember only parts of it so I am enjoying it now. The class
discussions in his course are being recorded by a local radio
station for later editing into eight half hour programs to be
broadcast in an educational series. I dispair at our saying
anything very educational since our discussions are generally a
mutual exchange of ignorance. However, since most of the people
in the country are not very well educated either, I suppose the
very fact that we have taken time to read the books will be of
some value.

    Ree has her weekly bridge group downstairs right now. There
are twelve of them and I have given up Ben Franklin in favor
of the typewriter since I can not here them as well with its
clickity-click going on. I still have eight of my interviews to
type. Ree made another icecream cake to serve this evening. She
is becoming quite an expert at it. I am to go down and offer to
serve drinks after they have finished their desert awhile. (It
is what they call a desert bridge, so they eat dessert first).
They keep at it until after midnight and then none of them can
sleep after they get home. I am usually asleep by then and can
not get to sleep afterwards either.
    [...]

                              72

So on that note I will close. My best wishes and love to Mother and yourself. Tomorrow is our long day with dinner seminar so it is not likely that I will write tomorrow.
                                        Love,
                                        Jack

Cumbie and Opal
Newton Street, June 1956

Dear Dad,

Today is a day off for me — I do not really mean a day off,
since I have more than I can do here at home, but I do not have
to go in to school. I had hoped that all of my Thursday's would
be free so that I could get a lot done on my thesis, but is
looks like this will be just about the only free one. They have
scheduled a lot of lectures and tours for all of the Thursdays
up to the time our thesis is due. It looks like a pretty rough
time for the next three months.

I got your Saturday letter and your Monday card. It is good
to hear from you so often. Remember me to Frank Padulla when
you see him the next time. We will have to pay him a visit too
when we get to Washington to stay. I plan to be very good about
visiting all the people we know there. I also plan to do a lot
of reading and a good deal of writing. We plan to be active in
Church and to keep our house in good condition. I also want to
spend more time doing things with the kids and helping them
with their education. When you add to this my determination to
do some office work at home, it will probably require a forty
hour day.

It's too bad Grandaddy is not more at home at Carroll Manor.
I certainly hope it is just a time of getting adjusted and that
he will come to enjoy it later on.

I suppose the trip down to Epiphany and St. Pats will be
a good arrangement for you and Mom since she is having her
letter transferred downtown. A trip downtown on Sunday morning
is not a very long one. I am impressed with the smallness of
Washington still. After seeing how many cities are so large
that you can not even pone out of the neighborhood without
a toll charge. Here in Boston we can not even call downtown
without a message charge. Even the time and the weather are a
charge because they are in the central district. It is the size
of the cities that do it. I have just finished Ben Franklin's
autobiography and the thing that is continually surprising to
me is to realize just how small the population was in his time.
It was easier to find a place in history then because there were
so few people. On the other hand Franklin would have found a
place for himself in any age.

This is the second day of lent and the thirty nine days to
go look pretty long in our house. Sharon and John have given
up TV. It is a good thing for John additionally because he
is behind in his school work. For Sharon it is a significant
sacrifice since she spends a good deal of time at it normally.

74

Linda and Ree have given up desserts and something else I do not recall at the moment. I am going to do what I should do all the time anyway and stop eating myself into an early grave. My real give-up item is coffee. I give up smoking too, but that is more to prove the thing is not a habit. All my pipes are pretty foul after being out of service that long.

We have had terrible weather. We had a little snow on the ground and then we had a real freak rain. It rained for several hours hard, and the whole time the temperature stayed in the low 20's. It was freezing and it was also standing because it was coming down so fast. Then it snowed more on top of that. On top of that Ree was parked at our dean's house where she had driven the Newton girls to a flower arrangement (she always drives if the weather or traffic is bad, being the better driver) and she got plowed in by the snow plow. We think the plow may have punctured the tire, or else it was defective , but she had just gotten well down along Beacon street when it went flat. A young fellow from MIT changed it for her in that terrible weather, so she got down to the Faculty Club for lunch okay.

Now I must get back to work. I will get Sharon to mail it for me.

My love to you and Mom,
Jack

[handwritten]

Had to go get Elmer out of a tree just as I was sealing this. He got himself out in the end but I was afraid the ice coating would make him fall. He is home safe now.

                                        Friday Evening
                                        February 13, 1959
Dear Dad,

    I got your card this morning — the Wednesday one. I was
just reading it over again and remembered I forgot to mention
the Northwest High Band to him. He is at Scouts now. Linda is
at dancing. Sharon is using John's microscope set, and Ree is
watching TV. I am taking a minute off from my studies.

    I had to read a book called SUBURBIA yesterday and today
and it got me to thinking about our house hunting. I am rather
looking forward to it. So is Ree, of course. If our plans go
as we hope, we will be in Washington with you four months from
today with the trailer partly unloaded, hopefully. Considering
all that I have to accomplish before then, it does not seem
possible.
    [...]
John did not like his school picture this year so we did
not buy the lot. We got just a few of the small ones — yours is
enclosed. He just does not like the expression on his face.

    Ree had her conference with Sharon's teacher yesterday. She
also got Sharon's report. Sharon is just a grade average in all
subjects except math, and she is below in that. The only bright
spot is that she is improving. Ree is giving special attention
to her multiplication tables and her spelling and we think she
will be okay. We are hoping it is just this upset year with
all three of them and that they will settle down next year and
bring home better grades.

    Tomorrow is the usual Saturday party for us, and of
course it is St. Valentines Day. The valentines from Mother
to the kids came yesterday and today, and are the only ones
they have gotten so far. I should have sent you and Mom my
Valentines wishes in the last letter, but I hope you had a
pleasant day. I will have to get out and do my shopping for Ree
sometime tomorrow — and she for the children — except for John,
who she got a model for today.

    And now I must see if I can not get a couple of hours on
my thesis before time for bed. I usually get to bed at midnight
and up at seven. Saturday's I try to sleep a little longer
because I lose a little sleep on Saturday nights. I have a
terrible time staying awake, even with the pills I take. On
this last book, the text was so difficult, I had to read most of
it out loud in order to keep awake.

It was too bad to have gone all the way out to see Grandaddy and found him asleep. He probably would have rather had you wake him. But it is also good to talk to the Sisters because they like to know the family is interested. It was that way with the girls in the convent in Key West. The Sisters are completely devoted to their work and the interest of the family must certainly make them feel better.

And now I really must get back to work.

Love,
Jack

WASHINGTON, 13
FEB 9
6 30 PM
1959

THE ACADEMY OF AMERICA
25th YEAR
1934-1959

U.S. POSTAGE 3¢
LIBERTY

John I. Cumberland, Jr.,

9 Whittelsey Road,

Newton Centre 59, Mass.

Monday Feb. 9, 1959.

Dear Jack.
Busy weekend. Took Mother to Ephiany at 11 and then I went to
St. Patricks to Mass and picked her up after church. We had
dinner at our regular cafeteria about 430 and stayed home the
rest of the day. This morning we went out to Bladensburg to
arrange to have the roof fixed, and on the way back stopped
by to see Frank Padulla-he thought we didn't stay long enough,
but I was getting tired by this time, so we came home. He
is improving some though he had a slight attack of pleurisy
last week. He enjoyed hearing about your short visit with
us and said your were "a good boy". Also we went to see
Dad at Carroll Manor Sunday and spent about half an hour there.
Last week Dad had some words with the Sxit Sisters and put on
his hat and coat and spent a few nights with Violet's mother.
Catherine and the Priest went over a nd I think straightened
things out.   Love to all.
                                    Fed.

78

Dear Dad,

   This is really going to be a super fast letter because I
have been getting more worried about the amount of time I am
getting into my studies. We are having regular course work
piled on top of our thesis work, and the thesis is taking a
back seat most of the time. But some of the fellows are finished
theirs already and I have not even started my analysis, much
less started to write. I will finish on time, of course, but
some other things may suffer, as well as the thesis, later on.

   We got a letter from Mother this morning. I guess I forgot
to mention that we will have the kids stay at Piney Point while
we are house hunting. We certainly will not want them under
foot, and there is more to occupy them at the beach. They are
at a very difficult age and the unrest of this year has made it
several degrees worse.

   We have had good clear weather to clear away most of the
ice and snow and the lakes and river are nearly clear. It even
begins to smell like spring if you have a wishful imagination.

   Ree is out to her bridge this evening. She was at a bridge
lunch at the faculty club yesterday too. Mrs. Allen was in this
morning for a visit — the mother of one of Linda's friends.
Linda had a school dance today. She is more than enthusiastic
about dancing these days. Sharon had her girl scouts today as
usual, and we have signed her permission slip for the trip to
Peterborough. It is a Boston College summer camp that BC allows
the schools to use during the winter. The girls do not take
any dresses or skirts so I guess they rough it. John was out to
Scouts tonight too.

   Now I had better get back to my books. I am reading a
book about the Senate called "The Citadel." I also read the
Constitution and Declaration of Indepence this week. I am
hoping that the rate of two books a week will ease up, but I
know they will just put something else in if it does.

                                        Love,
                                        Jack

Dear Dad,

Ree and the Kids are out seeing "Inn of the Sixth Happiness" and I am having an afternoon and early evening alone to study - -or rather work on my thesis. They have a wet trip of it because it has been raining steadily since this morning. It has taken most of our snow away but not all of it because it has been hovering just above freezing. Ree and I had hoped to go down to Trinity in town tonight to hear Chad Walsh — -one of the outstanding Episcopal writers. If the rain starts to freeze, or if they are late getting back, we probably will not go.

Tomorrow the children start back to school after their weeks vacation — much to our pleasure. The week was just about the end of Ree. The tension continues to build up as the year comes toward its end, and the children must feel it and are reacting by not doing the things they should.

John got hit by a basketball yesterday and I had to get him new frames for his glasses — charcoal gray for $9. What with his doctor bill for five dollars and the exray for ten, basketball is an expensive game. We are glad he has been able to take part in a sport this year, so it is well worth it. Sharon got to her overnight visit with Carol and to the Ice Follies. Linda has had two more baby sitting jobs. Ree and I were out to parties both Friday and Saturday this week. The pace is getting fast again in that respect.

We got the letter written on a towel. Your mention of DC income tax is a reminder that we will not be free of state tax once we take up residence in Maryland again. We are going to have to pay $114 Federal tax this year instead of getting some back like we usually do. Not having the house payments all year did that to us. It will probably be the same this year because we will not have a house for at least the first half of the year.

It is a blessing in disguise that you are home these days when Grandaddy needs someone to cheer him up. I had not realized that he had anything so serious as a blood clot, but I guess there are all degrees of seriousness in such a thing. Grandaddy, it seems to me, tends to be pessimistic about his health — you know how I always remind him of how he used to tell me it would probably be his last visit way back in my first year at Annapolis, nearly twenty years ago.

Well, it is nearly time to leave for church and the family is not back yet, so I guess we will not be going. At least that will be good for the thesis. Tomorrow is our long day this week since we have our dinner seminar on Monday instead of Tuesday.

Well, they finally just got back in time for us to leave, but I was not ready and we had to give it up. They would have stayed to see it over again if they had known.

Since they missed seeing a second show and Ree and I missed Chad Walsh, I feel obligated to get the most out of the time I have as a result, so I better dig into the thesis again.

Love,

Jack

Dear Dad,

I can tell by this stack of letters and cards that have arrived since I last wrote that it has been quite a while. I am on my way down the home stretch for my thesis and I do not seem to be able to get into my final stride. I have not been putting in more time than before, so that is not my reason for not writing more. It must be that I am just lazy. I did get in better than twelve hours yesterday though. But then I am well behind today because I spent too much time reading the new TIME.

Another thing that has sabotaged me this week is a bathroom faucet. It was more t han a simple washer that was causing the leak, but I had to do a lot of work and make a trip downtown before I found it out. I even had to overhaul the cutoff valve in the basement which evidently had not been used for many years. In the end I still had to call the plumber.

We have had a stretch of warm (relatively) weather lately and all the ice and snow is gone. It is raining now and Sharon came home at lunchtime soaking wet. Ree dried her out with the hair dryer and we sent her off for the afternoon bundled up in Johnny's Boy Scout poncho. She leaves for Peterborough, N.H. a week form Monday and we so mot want her to get sick before she leaves, or she will miss it. It is such a big adventure that missing it would be tradgic.

This has been a pretty busy week for us. I skipped a meeting yesterday so that I could get more time on my studies at home. I will have to do more and more of that until I get a little ahead. I have not even started to work on my thesis this week because of the load of other work and my goofing off part of the time. Now I have a paper on administration that I must get to work on since it is due in a couple of weeks. We also have our Canadian field trip before the rough draft of the thesis is due.

One thing the faucet trouble did for me in spite of the bad feature, was to send me on a trip into Boston's South Side. It is the Skid Row here — but it is not too terribly run down. The thing that I enjoyed was stopping a a men's bar there. There were a number of old men — half of the population there is single men over sixty — and it was a real old fashioned bar with wooden stools and TV and eight different kinds of draught beer, ale, and stout. I had a glass of ale, a hugh liverwurst sandwich with a side dish of pickled beets and onions for 30¢. Now I wish I had tried the stout, although I am told I would not like it.

Linda spent the night with a girl friend so we have not seen her since yesterday. Ree had to shop for slacks and a warm sweater for Sharon for her camping trip, and even Sharon is wearing clothes large enough for Ree now. John is a couple of inches taller than Sharon and it begins to look like he is at last gaining on Linda. It will be a great day for him — and the rest of us — when he finally passes her. He had his glasses broken last week playing basketball — but I seem to remember telling you about that.

    [...]

Now I am afraid I will have to get to that paper in administration. It is one of those things that I have put off as long as I can and yet it must be done.

We all send our love,
Jack

Sunday Evening
March 8, 1959

Dear Dad,

I am resting up from completing the first chapter of my thesis today. It is too late to get started on the next, so I thought I would write a few lines to you and turn it in. The one chapter I have done may be all wrong and have to be done over again after I show it to my thesis chairman. But at least it will be a step that has to be done that will be behind me.

The news about what happens here is generally how much I have gotten done on my work these days. It is a shame I have to neglect the family so much. We would love to have gotten up to see them taking the maple sap. Ree and I do get out to our weekly parties, but they seem like part of the school program by now. Last Saturday night — that would be last night — we played rummy instead of bridge for a change. I won the little paperweight prize.

The plumber came on Saturday but he knew less about the trouble than I did when he started. But he will be able to replace the faucet housing in the end and I would not have wanted to risk doing that myself.

We have had a very good week with John. He seems to have snapped into a good humor and has been quite cheery. Linda had a couple of nights with girlfriends last week and another babysitting job last night. Sharon is aiming for her Peterborough trip still and we put a pill into her each time she sniffles.

A funny thing happened while the family was out shopping and I was home studying. A little girl called who was babysitting over in Neeham. She couldn't contact the baby's mother and her own mother was out, so she just called a number to ask for advice. I told her not to make the baby eat the spinach and to just give her the bottle and put her to bed, but not to worry because nothing was wrong. She called back later and said that the baby went right to sleep. I have not had a problem like that in years.

Now to bed.

Love,
Jack

Friday Evening
March 20, 1959

Dear Dad,

I got your card today and am very glad to hear you are going
to be starting back to work next week — probably before you
receive this letter. Even though it may be quite tiring, I am
sure you will feel better at it. There is just a little more
than two months before your spring vacation, so you will have a
rest then.

The pressure of this home stretch has been pretty heavy this
last week. I got my last big term paper completed last Sunday
and turned in Monday morning. The only trouble is that it put
my thesis at a dead stop for more than a week at this very
critical time. I have got to start turning out written chapters
this evening. I have completed my reading and analysis and all
of this week's regular homework so that I have no excuse not to
start writing. I only have this weekend and next week before we
leave on our Canadian field rip. Then after the field trip I have
only one week before the rough draft of the thesis is due.

Sharon got home from her week at Peterborough this afternoon
we have been hearing all about it since she got home. She had
a wonderful time and will remember it all her life. They hiked
and cooked out and got in on mapel sugaring. We had three fine
letters from her in the short time she was gone. Sharon is the
best letter writer in the family.

Linda is off to her last dance of the year tonight. Sharon
had hers last Saturday and John has his tomorrow. One by one
the end of the year is coming for the various activities. Ree
spent most of the day setting up the first two of the final
rounds of parties that we will give. Our very last one will
be in the last week here; as will most of the rest of the
fellows. I have not given too much thought to the final week,
other than just knowing that your are looking forward to the
trip up. Now that it draws closer I can see that it will be an
extremely hectic week full of farewell parties among the Sloans
and the rest of the time taken up with packing. As best I can
see it right now your best bet will be to plan to get here on
Thursday. It will be the two most hectic days of the year, but
since it would only be two days, it hopefully won't tire Mother
too much. I still do not know what the situation is for tickets
to commencement, but I am hoping for the best.

Now I must get to my thesis. I have wanted to write several times this past week but each time I found myself under some immediate pressure to get something done — in fact, I did not get it all done and went to most of the classes unprepared. On top of that I have skipped the Thursday cases for the last two weeks.

Take it as easy as you can back at work and test up in the evenings.

All our love to you and Mom,
Jack

Dear Folks,

   You have probably wondered where I have been after my
regular writing habits of the past few months and now this
period of relative silence. This morning I turned in the rough
draft of the largest part of my thesis and I now feel like
I can rejoin the rest of the Human Race — which Ree claims
I have been out of for the past few weeks, and especially in
the last few days. As late as Saturday I just did not see how
I could pull it all together and ge a presentable whole, but
It finally came to me on Sunday morning and I sat down and got
a concluding chapter done that brought out my ideas on the
subject.

   Sunday was, of course, John's birthday. He wanted turkey,
so Ree got a small one and we all enjoyed it emensly. She
also made an ice cream cake. I took time off and we bowled four
stringsof candle pins. John and Linda do very nearly as well
as Ree and I. Sharon was off at a skating party. I broke 100
for the first time. We will probably do more of that because it
is fun that the whole family can have together. It is not too
expensive now that they have the automatic pin setters.

   Our present to John was his razor. It is an electric Schick
which Ree got at our favorite discount house for half price.
It should last him a long time. His moustach had gotten to the
point where it just had to go, but he had a hard time believing
that it was not a mistake, and that the razor was really for
him. Ree also got him new shoes, size 10 double A. That puts
him at my size except for the width, I had been wondering how
he came to be wearing my sox sometimes. I saw him writing some
letters so I guess he has written to thank you for his gift. I
lose track of who sent what but he was tickled with everything
he got. I am impressed by his growth at this time. This will
be the last time he is in boy's sizes. We have to give monthly
quotations these days. We will be lucky if he can wear his new
suit a second year.

   I suppose John mentioned the sciencefair in his letter. He
and Linda finally got their entry in and John got an honorable
mention. It was nearly the death of Ree because she had to
help them through their last minute crisis all alone with me
in Canada. We are not at all happy with the way they let it go
until the last minute — as they have done everything this year.

Another thing that bothers us these days is that Linda, and the other two to some extent, has started to treat the truth quite lightly, to the point where we have to think twice about anything they say about homework and schoolwork. Linda's trouble is along the exaggeration lines so that we hear her spinning long stories to friends that have hardly any basis in fact. What we can not understand is how she picked this up without being around Mother enough to find out where she gets it from. I am hoping both she and Mother outgrow it.

Our Canadian trip was a real pleasure. You can see from the card I sent what beautiful buildings they have for their capitol. I got a beautiful decanter of Czehoslvlkian crystal with small brandy glasses.

We have plumbers here now tearing the bathroom apart to replace the faucets. One of the faucet bodies went bad about a month ago and the only way to fix it is to take the whole wall out and replace all four faucets. We are hoping they will be able to complete the job this afternoon because we may have both bathrooms out of service until they finish. I am having a hard time staying away from where they are working because I would rather watch them than get to work myself.

Ree and I are going with a group to see "Destry Rides Again". tonight. It is a new show that is trying out here. We will have dinner at the Faculty Club first. I sure am glad I got my thesis in first. But I do have a lot of work that has piled up while I was working on that. I also have more of the thesis itself to do. So I had better get to work.

I am ever so glad that you are back to work and feeling fine.

All our love,
Jack

Oh, yes, I have written to Key West asking for their feelings about my transfering to the Bureau. I am still waiting to hear from them. I will know more what to do after I know how they feel. It shouldn't be long because I wrote a week ago.

                              Wednesday Afternoon
                              April 8, 1959
Dear Dad,

    I got your Sunday card yesterday, and was sorry, but not
surprised to hear you were tirid at the end of the second week.
I am finding that I just cannot keep up the pace I did during
the summer and even during the winter. It is not spring fever,
its just that any new pace gets tiring after you have been at
it long enough for the new to wear off.
    We had a short day today but I have not got as much done as
I hoped. I was delayed getting home and then Ree and I got to
talking. We are both on a diet now because she has never had to
watcher her weight, and even when she has in recent years it
only took a little moderation to take care of it. With Linda
watching her weight, we have a very weight conscious family. I
think Linda has the best success because she knows just which
skirts she has to lose weight to get into and she does it.
    I got a letter from my boss in Key West and he has given
me his blessing on my transfer to Washington. Now my only
problem is to find the job and go through the motions of getting
transferred and moved. I am not sure yet just how I will go
about it but I do not think I will force the issue just yet.
I will write to my friend in the Bureau, but I do not plan to
come down to see anyone before the trip in May unless they want
me to. That is only a little more than a month and a half off.
    My biggest problem for the moment is still my thesis. I
have a meeting scheduled for Friday afternoon and I have some
writing to so before then. After that meeting I must finish my
rough draft completely. I am hoping to have it ready for typing
by the twentieth which is a holiday up here. My typist wants to
do the typing that day.
    Linda is excited about a spectacular she is to take part in
at school. It is a musical that one of the teachers has written
for them.
    Today has been a real spring day as nice as any you could
ever hope for. I hate to see it end.
    Now I must get back to work.
                              All our love,
                              Jack

Friday Afternoon
April 10, 1959

Dear Dad,

This will be a very short letter. I do not even have the
writter up on the desk. Shenever I just have a few lines type I
leave it down here on the coffee table and squat down to type.
This way I am not tempted to go on and on because I get tired.

I have a stack of bills and other things — income tax, forms
that I take care of rather than Ree and those are the things I
am getting one of the kids to mail as soon as one of them is
home.

My thesis conference for today was called off so I have
another day to wait and another day to get the additional
chapter appendix written. But that just puts off the final rush a
bit longer.

Ree has gone with a couple of other girls up to a woolen
mill today. I think they have just gone shopping rather than
from any great interest in the textile industry.

Tomorrow we have a bridge party in the evening so it will be
a busy day getting ready. Ree had a coffee yesterday, though she
has a lot of inertia and should sail right through it.

I took her down toDergen park restruant in the market
last night and she had a huge roast beef. I think they have a
place like that down at the Florida Avenue market too. After
dinner we went to see "Some Came Running" out here at our local
theater.

Now I must finally get to that extra chapter.

All our love,
Jack

Dear Dad,

This has been another busy week since I wrote last, but now I can catch my breath again. I rewrote portions of my thesis and got it to my typist last Saturday morning. Then I had to work to catch up on the homework that I had let slide. I have one more chapter to finish and get to my typist and I have what she has typed so far back to proof read. That is still a lot of work but it does not seem so much now that the main part of the thesis is done. I still have a number of thank-you letters to write for my thesis trip as well as a paper in the finance course to do.

Sharon is spending several days with a friend down at the Cape. This is one of their eighth week vacations. Ree brought John and Linda and four of their friends down to the Faculty club for lunch today. Then they went to see "Shaggy Dog."

Last week the Sloan Fellows for next year were here looking for houses. There will only be one man from the Navy next year, I helped him as much as I could — mostly by loaning him the car. He could have taken this house, but she has raised the rent from $200 to $225 and he was able to do better in the next town over from us. A man from Shrievport, La. took our house. The year is certainly coming to an end in a hurry. We will be packing before we know it.

I guess it is a bad habit, but I have taken to smoking these little cigars that they make on the cigarette machines. They are a sort of cross between a cigar and a cigarette. I still smoke my pipes too, so this little den is full of smoke most of the time. You might like to try them, but they are probably too little for you. The ones called Trends are more like cigars (use more cigar tobacco). Than the Madisons.

I still have not heard anything from Washington on my job, but it is just possible that I may not hear before I go there late in May. I still do not contemplate any trouble. I will be having some kinds of mail forwarded to Newton street from now on but there is no need to send it up unless it is first class, in which case you can just forward it without additional postage.

Now I am either going to get back to work or go down and watch the US Steel Hour.

We all send our love,
Jack

Friday Afternoon
April 24, 1959

Dear Dad,

This is a very beautiful day here in Boston. I have not been out but Ree says it is hot and everything looks sunny and green. Later this afternoon we will be going to a cocktail, buffet, and square dance party. Ree has gotten a new, full skirt for it.

Much to our surprise we got a letter from Sharon this morning. She is probably the only 11 year old alive who would think to write a letter home on a 5 day trip to Cape Cod.

Ree went to a bridge party last night and I watched two ninety minute TV plays with the kids. With my thesis well in hand I find myself taking it easy — too easy I am afraid, because there are a lot of other things I must take care of.

We have received the notice of our graduation announcements and I just called the registrar because they left the comma out of my name as it will be on the diploma. I have to get my order in for the rental of my cap and gown now. We have only four more weeks of regular classes.

I have been glad to hear in Mother's last two cards how well you are feeling. You will certainly have no trouble in making the trip up in June — especially since you will have over a month to gain even more strength.

We are having a bridge party and dinner here tomorrow night, trying to catch up on our final obligations. We plan just one more general party on June 9. It will be one of many parties which will be held that last week.

I will take the final chapter of my thesis in for typing tomorrow morning, along with the corrections on the rest of it. She will probably do it over the weekend and give it to me on Monday. It is good to be in no rush at all because it is not due until a week from Monday.

Here is Sharon's school picture for this year. It is especially good so I am enclosing two sizes. You never know how they will turn out so you feel lucky when you get such a good one. I think I will take a minute to drop a line to Piney Point now since I feel just a little freer with my studies eased up.

All our love,
Jack

Dear Dad,

     This has been a busy week for us because it was the week of
the Sloan reunion. All of the Sloan fellows from previous years
— at least most of them — were here for a three day reunion.
We went to all of the activities also. There was a cocktail
party on Wednesday and some of us went to the Polynesian Room
for dinner afterwards. The Polynesian food is chinese for the
most part but there were some differences. On Thursday we had a
series of talks during the day while the women had a fashion
show and lunch. Our most interesting talk was by General Gavin.
He is the one who resigned in the missile controversy. We had
an evening of cocktails and dinner and a talk by both Sloan and
Killian. Then yesterday we had seminars with the old Sloans and
the faculty.

     John was sick yesterday and home from school but is back to
normal today. The rest of us are fine. John and Linda got their
reports last week. John's was good but not outstanding for him.
Linda had to C's in two out of her four major subject and her
two A's were in minors, so we are not pleased with her work.
They should do better once thay get settled.

     One of the old Sloans from the Navy in Washington had a job
prospect for me and I have written to the man he suggested.
This is a helpful development because it would be better to
have a selection of jobs rather than just the one that has been
promised me.

     I got my thesis in this last Wednesday in its final form and
got copies in the hands of all the members of my committee.
I even got one copy to the bookbinders. Now I only have to
arrange for my thesis examination and I am all done — except
for the thank you letters to the men who helped me and the ones
I spent the night with on my trip.

     Tonight we are going to a party and tomorrow we are going to
a dinner party and the Pops Concert afterwards. I still have a
financial report to complete as well as my regular homework and
a number of letters I must write. Then we have to get started
on the different things we need to do to be ready to move —
ordering the trailer is one big thing. Our arrangement to
unload the trailer in your garage is a great help in that we do
not need to worry about any arrangements at that end until we
get there.

I guess that is all I can think of for now. I will be
seeing you in three weeks when we come down for our Washington
field trip. I will let you know what my plans for that are as
soon as we have the schedule. I will probably stay at the hotel
with the group, but there will be some free time I am sure, and
I may stay over a day ortwo.

All send love,
Jack

                                   Monday Evening
                                   May 4, 1959
Dear Dad,

    Just a quick note tonight. I have gotten my thesis
examination scheduled for next week and that will just about
end that up — except for the than-yous I must write. I even
have some of them done. I have gotten the information on the
trailer and I will go in and put my deposit down on that on
June First. We have two more weeks of classes after this one,
and then we will be down for our Washington field trip. I think
we will be staying at the Presidential — or maybe he said the
Congressional. I am not yet sure when I will be able to see you
but I will have the schedule before we leave. I do know that we
have a dinner meeting Monday night with Judge Douglas so that I
will not be free then.
    We went to MIT night at the Boston Pops last night and we
had a real surprise. Danny Kaye, who has been a guest conductor
with them in the past, showed up and did some impromptu
conducting. He was a regular riot. He is a favorite of Ree's so
she was tickled to death. I enjoyed it immensely too. It was on
the front page of the morning papers.
    Ree was down to school today for the regular confferences
about John. He has done very well this year after all. The low
marks he has gotten were due mostly to the teachers' believing
that he would ease up if they marked him too easily. I guess
they know best but it gave us some unhappy times around the
house. A lot of credit goes to him for pulling himself out of
his grumpy spell.
    Now I have to stop in order to live up to my claim that
this is a quick note. Take care of yourself.

                                   With love,
                                   Jack

Dear Dad,

We just got the telegram about the success of your operation and we are all very happy about it. I hope it has not been too painful for you this time because even the simplest of operations leave you pretty darned uncomfortable. I will be looking for Mother's report on your convalescing and hoping that you will soon be home and able to travel. I forgot to ask the doctor how long he expected you to be in the hospital. I will be optimistic about it and send this to the house.

I just got back from putting a deposit on the trailer. I have to go up north of Boston to have it put on since they do not have one available closer. I did not want to take a chance on not being able to get the large 8x12 size van that I need. I will pick it up on Thursday and spend all of the rest of that day as well as Friday after graduation packing. Hopefully that will let us leave early on Saturday morning. Judging from past experience we may well have to spend part of Saturday packing also. I will have until quitting time Monday to get unloaded and return the trailer. The unloading should not take long because we will just be setting everything down on the garage floor.

John and Linda took their math finals today and both of them did well. Sharon's report for the last period came last week and she seems to be doing fine now. They should do okay next year wherever they are.

Yesterday we took a trip to Glouchester, Salem, and Marblehead. I think I enjoyed Salem the most because we say the Customhouse where Hawthorn worked and the House of Seven Gables.

Saturday night we were at the Divols' for a party and we were raided by the police for making so much noise singing. We figured that that made it the best party of the year automatically.

My trip home was not uneventful like most trips are these days. We were late taking off because the wind shifted and all of the planes had to go to the other end of the field. This make us nearly an hour late. Then there was a sea fog over Logan Airport and we had to land at Bedford Airport. The wives were waiting for us at Logan and we had all sorts of confusion before we finally met them at the Sheraton Hotel.

I have been trying to get two or three letters written
about jobs I am interested in, but different things have kept me
from it — television for one thing I am afraid. But now I must
be about that particular piece of business or I will find myself
without a job in a few weeks. I have three good leads right now
and I will develop more if I need to when I get down. I have no
classes at all today or tomorrow, so I will be able to get all
the letters written and get some other letters written that I
have to do in connection with my thesis trip.

Get well quick now and rest up. We all send our love and
our best wishes.

Love,
Jack

                                        Thursday Morning
                                        June 2 4, 1959
Dear Dad,

    I am hurrying to get a letter written to you so that John
can take it on his way to school. I am off for the rest of the
week so I do not have to go in today — I probably will not even
get dressed for the morning because I enjoy loafing around this
way.

    We got Helen's airmail letter yesterday morning, written
Tuesday afternoon. It was the first amplification we have had
since the telegram Monday evening, and it sounds like good
news. You seem to be recovering quickly. You must certainly be
home by now and feeling much better. We will be waiting to hear
whether you will feel up to traveling. Chuck Karrer brought me
two invitations yesterday so that I have them for sure. I was
pretty sure I would get them but I feel better now that I have
them in hand.

    I have been very busy since I wrote Monday night and this is
the first time I have really had to relax and write some more.
Even now I am rushing to get the letter ready for John to take.
It isn't a big rush since I will just stop when John leaves and
send what I have written. Last night Ree and I went down to the
Faculty Club for the last weeping hours. Those are the times
when they have all the drinks for 40¢ and the biggest crowd is
there. We had dinner there too. Yesterday I was down at the IBM
building to play the management decision game with my group.
We divided into three mock companies and made decisions on a
simulated market for our products. Our decisions were fed into
the IBM 650 and then we repeated the process. We did eight
quarters all day.

    Here is John. Hope you are all well quick,
                                        Love,
                                        Jack

Dear Dad,

I am writing first thing in the morning again so that John can mail this for me on his way to school. We have nearly come to the end of this series of letters. Our mail here has started to come to Newton Street. There was no news about you in yesterday's mail so we have still only heard up to Monday afternoon.

I spent all day yesterday getting odds and ends on my desk cleared up and I still have a long way to go. I called Key West to talk to my boss there about spending some time in Washington, but he was on leave until next Thursday. I will call him then because I am sure there will be no problem about it.

Yesterday evening we went down to school to see a couple of plays the children were putting on. The only reason we went was that John and Linda were in the orchestra. Ree had never seen the orchestra before. One of the plays was pretty good but the other was long and not so good. The audience, both children and adults, was terrible. You could hardly hear the orchestra over them. It must be this modern schools system or maybe just the times.

It was good to get into bed early for once last night. We have been going pretty steady every evening lately. I lose a lot of time in the morning when we are out late and I sleep late. Tonight we have a party down at the Faculty Club. We are hoping that it will not last too long because we plan to get up early and go down to the Cape and take the ferry from Wood's Hole over to Nantucket and Martha's Vineyard. We will have Sharon's friend Carol with us for the weekend. It will be our last trip around here.

Except for next Thursday when we will be packing the trailer, today is my last day off of the year here. We have evaluation meetings Monday, Tuesday, and Wednesday next week. Ree and I have our party Tuesday night and the farewell dinner is Wednesday night. There is a farewell party Monday night that we are going to skip because Linda is in her spectacular that night. We might have tried to see the dress rehearsal of the spectacular and gone to the party, but it is pretty expensive and there have been just too many parties all in a row lately. There are always the same people there so they all get to be about the same thing.

I am glad the Goldupps were able to come up and be with you for the operation. I suppose that you are home and they are back at Piney Point by now. The children, John and Linda at least, are in the middle of their final exams and are looking forward to the carefree days at Piney Point. It will not be long but it seems that way to them right now. They were all delighted to hear that you came through the operation successfully. We had explained that it was not a serious operation, so even our chief worrier, Sharon, did not get worried about it.

It is getting toward time for John to leave and I have long since run out of news. I will drop another line after the mail comes with more news.

With our love,
Jack

Dear Dad,

    We are going to eleven o'clock service this morning so I have some time to write before we leave. I can mail this on the way and you will have it on Monday probably.

    Our trip to Nantucket yesterday turned out to be a trip to Martha's Vineyard. It was just as well because the longer trip to Nantucket would have gotten us back much later and we had just as much fun with what we did. We got a late start and then had trouble with the car. Fortunately we found a Ford place in Buzzard's Point that did a fine job on the whole ignition system. They replaced the fuel pump even though it was not causing the trouble because it was pretty worn and I did not want to take the time to have them put my old one back on after it was changed in the trouble shooting procedure. The real trouble was the coil — which the Newton Ford place had replaced just last Fall.. He also set and cleaned both my points and my sparkplugs, so I am all set for the trip down next week.

    The ferry trip over to the Island was just a 45 minute trip. We had three hours over there. We hired a cab to take us around to see the island then we had dinner there. The island is just a summer tourist place today, although it was once a great whaling port. The houses there are almost all made with the plain white pine shingles — ever the very expensive ones. There are many very expensive homes which the owners only keep open for a few months each year.

    Sharon's girlfriend Carol is spending the week with us — or rather the weekend. I guess she will be our last little guest of the year. The are having some kind of farewell party for Sharon today at one of her friends' houses.

    There was no news in the mail yesterday. I only got my check and a magazine. I will have my check sent to Newton Street after this. In fact, I plan to send out all of our change of address cards today and all of our mail will be coming to Newton Street.

That is all for now. I hope you are feeling well and are pretty well recovered from the operation. Although we are hoping that you will be able to make the trip up, be sure that you are strong enough before you attempt it. We are all ready for you — actually there is nothing to do to get ready. John will have his room pretty well cleared out by Thursday — but then we will plan the sleeping after you get here and know where you will be the most comfortable. Anything will fit into our plans since the last planned event is the farewell dinner Wednesday and we are free after that.

All our love,
Jack

610 Murray Lane
Annandale, Virginia
December 1, 1959

Dear Friends,

WE HAVE MOVED AGAIN AND ARE SENDING OUR LETTERS OUT EARLY BECAUSE
WE DON'T WANT TO MISS HEARING FROM YOU THIS YEAR, EITHER. SO PLEASE
NOTE THE ABOVE ADDRESS!

Our wonderful, crazy, eventful year as an M.I.T. Sloan family is
a thing of the past and we aren't sure that we will ever be the same
again. We are s ure the other Sloan Alumni reading this must feel the
same way. The months following our Newton Centre leave-taking have
been quite eventful, too, and all of the Cumberlands are looking
forward to a more relaxed way of life after the Holiday Season--just
for a change.

Our last months in the Boston area were as exciting and interes-
ting as the first ones. Our trip to New York in December more than
lived up to expectations. In that one week-end, we not only saw
"Bells Are Ringing", but got into the Saturday matinee of "My Fair
Lady" and the evening performance of "Music Man". Also saw the
Christmas show at the Music Hall, the show at the Latin Quarter, and
had dinners at the 666 Club overlooking the heart of the city just as
the lights were coming on, and the next night at Asti's in Greenwich
Village, complete with singing waiters. All in all, a week-end not
to be forgotten.

After Christmas we all made a hurried trip to be with Jack's
Dad in Washington while he broke his 60 year record of never being in
a hospital. Then back to MIT to grind out the thesis, to be graduated,
and to leave Boston and return to the real world.

The Summer and Fall were eventful too, but it is difficult to
say what the events were. The children joined their maternal grand-
parents for a carefree summer at Piney Point, Md. Ree and Jack spent
a month in Washington, then a month in Key West, then back to
Washington for three months--with a stopover in Nassau.

We took an apartment in Fairfax County just in time to get the
children into their permanent schools. It has meant a lot of driving
for Ree, but it should all be over by the time you read this. We will
be in our new house on Murray Lane.

Jack's new job is in the Pentagon office which puts the Navy's
Research and Development budget together. This poses a problem for
the children who have always been able to explain that their father
designed mines, or tested torpedoes, or went to school. Now they have
trouble explaining what he does--he even wonders about it himself.

It is easy for anyone to say what Ree does. She drives three
children around all day and most of the evening. We have high hopes
that this will end now that we are moving onto the school bus route
and also getting a driver's license for John.

Besides learning to drive, John is back to marching in a good
band at Annandale High and working his way through the tenth grade.
He has had his spurt of growth this past year and he needs only six

more inches to reach his announced goal of 6' 2".

Linda has settled into what we hope are here lifetime dimensions--
her mother's dress size, but with enough height to make the basket-
ball team. She is in the ninth grade at Annandale High and enjoying
more than ever her flute and the advantages that come with a brother
in the grade ahead of her.

Sharon is in the second of her three years as a senior. The
seventh grade is the senior grade in Annandale Elementary just as the
sixth grade was for her last year. Next year she will be in the
eighth grade senior class in the new Edgar Allan Poe Intermediate
School. But it is the year after that that interests our Tom Sawyer
Sharon--the year she can be a varsity cheer leader for the Northern
Virginia Chapions. Both girls are looking forward to having a room
of their own at last, AND A DISHWASHER.

We still have Elmer, the World's Best Cat. After two years, we are
still trying to find that one fault. At present however, he is re-
siding at Piney Point, Maryland with Ree's parents. Our travels
this summer and our apartment life since September just didn't fit
into his plans. He has paid us visits and we him, and as soon as
we are settled in our new home he will be back with us permanently.
We're sure he'll be happy about that--but will undoubtedly miss all
that sand at the beach.

This is a year of transition for us and our letter seems as
unsettled to us as we feel ourselves. But the year ahead looks like
a calmer one and we hope next year's report on the life and times of
the Cumberlands will be an intimate picture of the typical American
suburbanite family. We will add one comment about geography before
we close. Our location here in the Washington Area has place us
in a location where many of you are likely to come. This letter goes
only to those families who are expected to stay at 610 Murray Lane
when they visit the Nation's Capital. We can sleep several adults
and untold numbers of kids, and we look forward to many visitors in
these next few years.

We wish you a Merry Twelve Days of Christmas and three hundred
sixty-SIX days in a Happy New Year.

                                    THE CUMBERLANDS
                                        JACK
                                        REE
                                        JOHN
                                        LINDA
                                        SHARON

AVE ATQUE VALE

SUNDAY MORNING BEFORE CHURCH
April 5, 1953

My godlike father with all his hair
is planted with his subjects on his lawn:
my mother in her slender suit, like Hera
in spitcurls; my godmother in final bloom,
dimpling for my uncle hunched over
the camera; we three kids arranged in front
like caryatids, supporting all their pride:
my sister with her golden hair and skirt
too long, my brother beaming —
his father's heir, the favored, only son.
And I — on tiptoes, straining to exceed
my brother's height, the only solemn face.
My intention drills the camera: taller,
smarter, taller, stronger — lovelier
than Hera, even. More solid than the god.

My Washington Monument

June 15, 2017

I sit in the dark with a monument
stilled to white marble.
His hands are folded over his chest,
his cheekbones jut from his face
like frozen waves.
I am grateful his eyes closed
on their own.
His hands are still warm.
I kiss his forehead.
He is cold, colder.

In the dark I wonder
if a subject without a king
is free.
Is an orphan free?
His last word
was his nickname for me:
Sherry.
What little girl has a parent
for sixty-nine years?
Suddenly, as I sit there,
I see an old woman.
In what sense
am I free?

Sharon Cumberland is Professor Emeritus of English at Seattle University, where she directed the Creative Writing Program and taught poetry writing and American literature. She has published scholarly work in orality and literacy studies, new media, and fan fiction. She spent her first sabbatical year in the Media Studies Program at M.I.T. Her chapbooks are *The Arithmetic of Mourning* from Green Rock Press, *Sharon Cumberland Greatest Hits* from Pudding House Publications and, with Denis Caswell, *CCausmwbeelrlland,* from Floating Bridge Press. Her poetry books are *Peculiar Honors* and *Strange with Age,* both from Black Heron Press. Her poems have been widely published, and she has won many awards and residencies. She lives in Shoreline, Washington with her husband, the scholar, editor, and letterpress printer James T. Jones.

The text and titles of *Found in a Letter 1959* are set in Minion Pro. The book was printed on Domtar Lynx 80-pound white opaque ultra-smooth paper by Bookmobile in Minneapolis, Minnesota.